DEATH MATTERS

GEORGIA SIMONIS

authorHOUSE®

AuthorHouse™
1663 Liberty Drive, Suite 200
Bloomington, IN 47403
www.authorhouse.com
Phone: 1-800-839-8640

First published by AuthorHouse 1/8/2009

ISBN: 978-1-4389-4059-5 (sc)
ISBN: 978-1-4389-4058-8 (hc)

Printed in the United States of America
Bloomington, Indiana

This book is printed on acid-free paper.

I dedicate these writings with loving memories to truth and justice; to my parents, Robert and Mary Simonis, for the incredible job they did raising all thirteen of us kids and many others, too. I am proud to be their daughter—
a true Simonis.

ACKNOWLEDGMENTS

I would like to acknowledge my daughter-in-law, LaRay, for all her helpful assistance in the computer preparation of this book. Without her I might still be stuck!

I also would like to thank my family and my husband, Kim, for his patient understanding and the love he has always shown me in all the various endeavors I have taken on. I am grateful and love you all.

TABLE OF CONTENTS

Part Four

PREFACE

The following story is inspired by true events. Because the events escalated into the International News Service, names of some officials have been changed to avoid embarrassment or slander. It is an emotional and thrilling story of a family that believes in and lives their personal responsibility, within every aspect of their lives, from birth to death. It tells of a large family's love and devotion to one another, and the idea of a true family unity and what unity means to them. It is written with the hopes that it will awaken and enlighten some of our society to the rights and wonders that death has if we are open to it. Life is precious, and death has the same value to our being. Death should be just as precious to us because it is a part of life.

We, as a society, have been programmed to pass most of our personal responsibilities off to some agency that will "take care" of whatever the circumstance calls for. This family has taken on the task of caring for their deceased family members. Many things have been experienced by members of this family after a death that have led the author to become a believer in the spiritual afterlife. The author has found that by taking care of her deceased family members, clear through to the disposal of the body, a new path of spiritual thinking has been accepted by her and her family. The clarity of life after death that these experiences have brought to this family, and the spiritual rewards they realized, are beyond any beliefs they had known. Sometimes, in the time after someone has died, you might get to experience a little of this "spiritual life after death" if you are open to it. This book just might make you a believer in this phenomenon.

INTRODUCTION

When I was twelve years old, I remember running across the street as fast as I could;

I was tripping and crying, not knowing where I was going. I just had to run; my mother had just told me that my favorite aunt [whom I was named after] was dying of cancer. I loved my aunt. I called her Aunt Juju. I loved her with all my heart, and I could not comprehend or imagine that she would not be around me or her children for the rest of my life. At that age, I probably didn't know what life was. But I did know what death was. The questions were loud in my mind; what would happen to her little children if she were not here to raise them? What would I do without her? So I ran and ran until I could not run anymore. I collapsed in the neighbor's yard, fifty feet from my door. When I sat up, I thought for an instant, *how did I get here?* It didn't matter; that horrible thought came back to me. My Aunt Juju was going to die.

Not long after I found out about my aunt's illness, I was babysitting a family friend's child when I awoke to the telephone ringing. I overheard the woman, Micky, whom I was working for, crying. This raised my curiosity. When the child I was babysitting wanted me to play with her, I couldn't play. Something was wrong. Was Micky crying? She had come to check on us only minutes before. So I went into her room and asked her if the call had been for me. Micky sat me down and very bravely gave me the news that Aunt Juju had passed away during the night. I couldn't believe it, but at the same time, I knew it was true. I had sensed it when the phone rang. Immediately, I wanted to go home to my mother. I needed my mother now. I needed her warmth and understanding, yet I wanted to stay where I was. I loved being away from home; there was always some chore for me to be doing there with a big family. Working away from home made me feel free and grown up. But when something as personal as this happens, I want the security of my mother. I started to cry; all I could think about was wanting to see my aunt. Wonderful thoughts went through my head of all the many times we were together and all the great things she had done with me that made me feel loved by her. Micky told me we would go tomorrow to see her when the funeral home had more time to prepare my aunt for viewing. Viewing? What did that mean? The following day, Micky took me to the funeral home to visit Aunt Juju.

To a child of twelve, this was the scariest thing I had every experienced. Again I thought, I wish I had gone home. Where was my mom? Micky spoke to a man that met us at the front door.

She said, "We are here to see Georgia Moore."

He replied, in a morbid manner, "This way, please," and he escorted us to a room down the hall.

Looking through the open doors in the hallway as we walked, I saw one room with three caskets in it. I can still remember the wood-colored caskets with white, shiny, satin linings. Each one was a little different. The man opened a closed door, and there was my favorite aunt, lying in one of those same caskets. She was very still looking in a blue flowered dress, and she had makeup on her face that looked different than that she had worn in life. A curtain was swaying behind her coffin. I was shocked and frightened at her appearance. I could not take my eyes off of her, yet I didn't want to look at her. I wanted to hide my head or just turn around and run. I felt as though a heavy presence was in the room. My breathing became labored; I didn't know what was happening to make me feel this strange way. I closed my eyes, and soon I noticed I didn't feel afraid anymore. I opened my eyes and a warm sensation went through me. I was confused. This was my first encounter with death, and what was it I was feeling? After a few minutes, I sat down on a bench that was the only other thing in the room. Micky then left the room, and I was left there alone with this dead person. As much as I loved and trusted my aunt, I was afraid again to move in this situation. I remembered thinking how scared I was. I wanted to leave, but I was afraid to move. Most of all, I was afraid my aunt might move.

When Micky came back into the room, I was more than ready to leave. Another feeling was erupting in me; we were leaving my aunt here alone, and it didn't seem right. I felt like I was abandoning her by leaving her in this place alone. It was cold and frightening here. I had helped take care of her for so long, it seemed wrong and unnatural to see her here and to leave her in this lonely, strange place alone. At twelve, I had no power to resist what was being done with Aunt Juju, so with a heavy heart, I took ahold of Micky's hand and left the room.

This is how I think, sometimes more than not, most of us as human beings react to death. If we are left alone with the dead, they may scare us a little. When death comes, we are conditioned to conform to what we believe we have to do. We call a funeral home to let them come and take care of our departed loved ones. In our current culture, it doesn't cross our minds to think of taking care of our departed loved one ourselves.

This is my story experienced through my father's nine-year struggle with illness and eventually death. My family and I wanted to honor my father's last wishes to keep him at home after his death and to bury him in a plain pine casket on "The Property" that he worked and loved so much. Through carrying out his wishes, I was given the spiritual confidence and moral determination that changed me for the rest of my life. By following my dad's wishes, my family and I endured many emotional and physical hardships.

This story is of an overzealous coroner and an unwarranted police siege of my family and me, which ultimately changed my thinking and my way of life. I could say now it was for the betterment of my life, but at the time it occurred, it was dangerous, frightening, and unlawful.

My name is Georgia, and I am the third child of eleven children born to Robert Simonis, my father, and Mary Simonis, my beautiful mother. Growing up, I always considered myself to have been "special" to my dad.

Bob, as he was called by most people, was born in Pablo, Montana in 1918. He was told by his parents that he was the first white child born on the Flathead Indian Reservation. His father, Walter, was the son of immigrants that came to this country from Germany in 1863. They were proud people, and very proud of their American citizenship that they received a short time after they arrived in America.

Bob's parents came from Montana down through Idaho and Oregon on a covered horse-drawn wagon and settled in Anderson, California with seven children when he was twelve years old. His father worked in the hills above Redding, California as a logger. Bob grew up living an outdoorsman's life. He was a logger with his father and brothers. He knew the forest and the ways of the woods like the back of his hand. I remember many stories of how he was called to help search for someone who may have been lost in the woods, or when someone called just to ask for his assistance in a possible location where someone might be. He was looked up to, and his word was gold. He was an excellent logger, very conscientious and knowledgeable about the environment, an expert hunter, and just an all-around nice guy. He was a man of few words, but people said that "his eyes and smile said it all."

Bob enlisted in the navy and served his country in WWII and the Korean War. He served a total of nine years in the service. I was born soon after he finished his last tour.

Bob met Mary Miller through his youngest brother, Kenneth. Mary was friends with Kenneth. One evening, Kenneth, his wife, and Mary went to the Temple Lounge in town for some music and dinner. As they came in, Kenneth was excited to see his older brother, Bob, sitting at the end of the bar. Bob had been living out of town so it was a pleasant surprise for Kenneth to get to see him. Bob jumped up from his seat to receive his brother, and Kenneth introduced Mary to him. While they were trying to get a table for dinner, Bob kept interrupting and insisting that they have a drink with him at the bar.

Mary later said, "Bob reminded me of a drunken sailor."

That night, Bob represented everything Mary disliked in a man. She thought he drank too much, he rode a Harley Davidson motorcycle, and his appearance was sloppy and untidy. He obviously wasn't the fastidious Mary Miller's type.

Mary was appalled at her first meeting with this man, so she was upset with herself for not being able to forget about him.

She said one time to me, "I don't know what attracted me to your dad. He wasn't my type at all. I was planning to be a spinster."

Did it have something to do with those piercing blue-green bedroom eyes as she called them? Bob had sandy brown hair and was five-foot-eleven, 180 pounds. He carried a sexy smirk on that handsome face that one didn't easily forget. Even though he was a little drunk at their first meeting, she still noticed he was an exceptionally handsome man of twenty-nine.

Bob couldn't forget Mary either. Drunk or not, he knew he had to see this lady again. He wondered why his brother introduced her to him. She wasn't his type; she was different from all the women he'd met or been with before. She was tall with blue eyes and incredibly slim. Very reserved acting with beautiful long curly black hair; a genuine beauty, he thought. Most women, because of his good looks and charismatic personality, flocked to Bob and devoured his attention. But Mary paid no attention to him and this intrigued him. He was afraid from that moment of his feelings for her. He had to ask himself if he could live without this woman. Was she the woman he was going to marry? That was a funny thought. He didn't think of himself as the marrying type. Where did that come from? All he knew was he had to see her again, and he did, a week later. This time he was completely sober.

After a few months of long-distance courtship, Bob was working in Quincy, California while Mary lived in Redding, California; they got married in May 1947 in Reno, Nevada. Mary's sister and her husband accompanied them for a quiet ceremony and a beautiful dinner. After marrying, they rented a house in Quincy where Bob was working as a logger, and Mary was happy to stay at home taking care of the house and her new husband. A year later, they moved to French Gulch, California where Bob's parents lived. They were also close to Mary's family. This was a welcome move for both of them. Their first child, a son, was born in 1949. They named him Walter after Bob's father. Granddad Simonis called him Little Si.

By 1955, Bob and Mary had had five children in six years. Mary decided she had to have a bigger home that was closer to town for her growing family. The family had outgrown the house trailer that they had lived in. Since she had never been able to get Bob to commit to buying anything more than the trailer they lived in, Mary took it upon herself to find a house that was big enough for all of them, and then she let Bob know about it. They used Bob's Cal-vet loan to buy that home. That was the beginning of Mary's unique wisdom into taking more control over the decisions for their family. By 1967, Bob and Mary had their last child, Hester, number eleven. They had also taken on the responsibility of raising Mary's sister, Aunt Juju's, two small children after she passed away. They always said one more or one less didn't make any difference when you have that many children.

For many years, I have wanted this story brought to light and my family's side of the story told. In my hometown at the time, my family received a tremendous amount of support for what we did when my father died. Whenever the occasion arises to tell the story, people are very interested. Their reactions range from amazement to total disbelief. This story at the time was reported across the world. My sister, Margaret, was visiting New Zealand in 1981 when she was introduced to a lady that connected her last name with the same name as a story she had read about in America a year earlier; regarding a family who would not give up their dead father's body after his death. This same scenario had been reported back to the family from other places also. I have always felt that what happened at the time needed to have the family's side of the story exposed. Now, with all the memories and emotions that writing this has brought back to the surface, I realize that the time is right for people to be excited and interested in taking care of their deceased loved ones and in the spiritual aspects of what can come from this experience. These are some of my reasons for this book, and it has been a long time coming. My family is of the utmost importance to me. I am thankful for so many things that my ancestors and past have contributed to my family's unity and power. So for me, in all matters that involve my family, "Death Matters."

PART ONE

Chapter 1
Growing Up

My father was an extraordinarily hard-working man. He was a good provider for his family. He never did a great deal for himself in the way of fun; his family always seemed to come first for him.

"When you have thirteen mouths to feed, there isn't a lot of time for yourself," he used to say.

He never complained about what it took to raise us kids. If there was something that we needed, he was the first to help us get it. Most things my father did, he did the hard way, never asking for any help from anyone.

My mother used to say, "He will drive fifty miles instead of asking for help or using the telephone for some little thing he needs."

Many of the adventures my brothers, sisters, and I did as kids, did not involve my father. He, as I said before, was usually working, cutting wood, or hunting. Most of his hunting or cutting wood was to support the needs of his family. I was on the swim team when I was young, and I have a few memories of times when we were going on a swim team trip and my father decided to go with us. That was always special to us kids to have him with us. I am sure Mother appreciated the help, too. We would camp at places like Patrick's Point, on the coast, or once up the coast into Eugene, Oregon. We always camped because of the number of us and Dad would cook for us.

I knew my father worked hard for his family when I was growing up. I never realized how hard until I was grown. When I was young, I didn't expect a lot of attention from Dad because I knew he worked most of the time, and he was tired when he came home. He usually was in bed by eight o'clock, up at 3:00 a.m. and off to work. On some evenings, it was difficult for us kids to be quiet at such an early hour, and if we got too loud, Dad would come raging out of his bedroom to see where all the noise was coming from. If that happened, we all scattered. We didn't want to be caught being the one who woke him up. We would receive one warning and that was all we needed.

My mother was the authority figure. She did most of the discipline in the family, and it was only once in awhile that she would require any help from Dad. As we got older, she sometimes called on him to discipline us, and it usually only took a word from him. If he had to react to mother's calls, we knew that meant business. I can remember just disregarding Mother's request to do something but I made sure that Dad's requests were followed to the letter.

I was fifteen when my parents remodeled our house. Most of my family was staying at my aunt's house—a block from ours. Dad was remodeling so he stayed at our home. It was summer so it didn't matter if walls weren't complete. Redding weather was very warm and it seemed quite fun, as if we were camping. I was staying with

Dad one night, when a friend stopped by and asked me to go along for the ride with him to take another friend home.

I telephoned my mother at my aunt's house and asked her, "Can I go with Gary [whom I had a crush on] to take a friend home?"

It was ten in the evening.

She said, "No, you are to go to bed."

Being fifteen, I decided for myself, since mom was not at the house to know what I was doing, and Dad was asleep, I would go anyhow and she would never know the difference. How can mothers know so much? It was a beautiful full moon evening, and I listened to the guys talk as we drove. I never considered I would get caught. Driving up our street as Gary turned the corner, the first thing I saw was my mother's car in the driveway. Then through the kitchen window, I saw my mom with my dad. We were only gone about an hour, but I knew I was in trouble.

I panicked and told Gary, "Just drop me off and drive away."

I knew that this was going to be bad for both of us. Gary wouldn't do as I asked, and by the time he pulled into the driveway, my dad was already out the door with my mom right on his tail. I opened the door of the car and jumped out, hoping Gary would drive away before my dad could get to him. My father picked up the first thing he saw, which happened to be a long piece of wood.

He grabbed me by the arm, gave me three swats on the rear end, and said, "Get in the house!"

I ran toward the house, looking back to see what my dad was going to do to Gary. Gary just sat there in his car and waited.

Dad went to the driver's side of the car and yelled at Gary, "Leave now and you better never come back around this house again."

I was so embarrassed I thought I would die right there. But you know, the next day I spoke to Gary on the telephone, and he said he respected my parents for caring enough to reprimand both of us for ignoring their orders. At the time, I really didn't understand Gary's attitude. I thought he should have been as mad as I was at my dad. I learned a lot about love and respect from that evening. Later on, I understood my parents for the physical choice my dad used on me that night, which made me think twice about whatever it was I was doing in the years to come. About a week later, Gary was welcomed back to the house.

Being a logger in Northern California meant you usually were unemployed during the winter months. I thought it was so neat to have Dad at home more. This was the time when I learned more about him. He did little wonderful things that left me with lifelong warm memories. One Christmas when I was about seven, all of us older kids got new shiny bikes on Christmas morning from Santa Claus. The weather was warm and sunny that morning, so after opening presents I decided to try that new shiny blue bike out. Well, Dad saw me struggling in the gravel to ride it and came out to help me. He took me out on the street and gave me a push. Not knowing how to ride very well, I went straight over the handlebars head first onto the street. He ran to me, picked me up, and carried me bawling into the house. I remember putting my head into his chest blaming Santa Claus for giving me that bike. Another time when I woke up for school, and Dad was home from work because it was raining, he was cooking breakfast for us kids; his specialty was "hotcakes and eggs." That was very special. It was as little as getting a ride to school, when I could have walked, but Dad would start that little red Jeep and take me. It was coming home to homemade bread, a big pot of red beans, and the whole family sitting down to the huge table to eat it. Those memories I can't replace or forget. As tough as he was, and he was tough, his heart was tender.

Being the great hunter Dad was, as a child, I ate a lot of wild game through the winter. My Great-Uncle Felix wrote a poem to honor Dad and gave it to my brother Si for his first birthday, after his first hunting trip with Bob.

He was so thrilled and impressed with his hunting skills, that he said, "It inspired the poem."

It was quite a tribute to my father's knowledge of the woods and courage towards animals.

My uncle published this account of the hunting trip he took with Bob in the late forties, twenty-five years after he wrote it.

He said, "Bob is still the greatest outdoorsman in these parts that I have had the honor to meet."

It goes like this:

Listen, my lad, and you shall hear
How your old great-uncle once hunted deer.
I had no gun, which of course sounds strange
Way up on top of the Trinity Range,
But, of course, my boy, always at my side
Was your pappy, Robert, as my friend and guide.

"Twas a wonderful trip; all chucked full-o-thrills
Jes' Robert-n-me in the Trinity hills.
I'd begin to think we's down on our luck
When all of a sudden I spotted a buck.

Ah! Here's the end of our vigilant hike.
Then Bob said, "No! That's only a spike."
"Well, spike or buck, a fawn or a doe,
It looks like deer; that's all I know!"
But Bob said, "Yes I know; that's the pity.
It happens to all the green-horns from the city.
If it wasn't for guys so fast on the trigger,
We'd have more game and a lot more bigger.
So take it from me, never be trigger happy."
Yep, son, that's a lesson I learned from your pappy.

Well, we both sat down in the morning's hush
When all of a sudden in the underbrush
Was the darndest noise I had ever heard
But your pap jes' laughed-n-said, "only a bird."

Then I sat back down in the morning breeze,
And I laid Bob's rifle down across my knees;
While off in the distance we could see a doe,
In her graceful way, up the mountain go.
Then right close by came a sudden sound,
And a buck came by with a leap and a bound.
His horns were forked like an old hat rack.
Well, I thought for a minute I'd blow my stack.
Yes, I dropped the rifle and started to point,
I act'd like a logger in a burlesque joint.
Then Bob said, "Hey won'tcha' watch him run!"
"Come on, old boy, gi-me back that gun!"

Well, I scrambled around in the gravel-n-sand
Till I got the rifle in yer pappy's hand.
Then he blazed away at the fleeting deer,
And we watched him stumble, then disappear.
Well, I started out in a racehorse lope
Till I came to the edge of the mountain slope,
But Bob jes' waited and I heard him say,
"Take it easy, old boy, jes' leave him lay."
Well, I looked at Bob with a quizzical frown,
"Who'r you kiddin'? Do you mean he's down?"
"He's down all right and I don't mean if,"
"But he'll get up fore he gets too stiff."

Well, I'll be a brother to a hound dog pup
If that deer didn't get right up.
Yep, jes' exactly like yer pappy said,
Not ten feet away was the rascal's head.

Then the deer made a lunge thru' the brush-n-sticks
But ole Bob pulled down with the thirty-ought-six.
He hit that critter smack-dab in the head.
The deer didn't fall, but he leaped instead.
Then Bob made a dive for the wounded buck.
To do that, Laddie, took plenty-o-pluck.
Bob went right over and the deer came next.
I'm standing by but I'm plum perplexed.
Never saw such a battle in all-o-my life,
Till finally ole Bob got-a-hold of his knife.
It was soon all over with a lurch and a quiver.
The next thing I know'd Bob throw'd me the liver.

Then we started the steep climb back to the top
And I thought sure-as-shootin' I was going to flop.
But ole Bob, too, was as tired as I.
And I guess by now, you can reason why.
For you see, he carried the deer, my lad,
While the gun and the liver was all I had.

Dad could always be counted on during the winter rainstorms to help the neighbors get across the bridge. He would take that little Jeep, hitch up a chain, and pull their cars through the rising water to safety.

I think I can speak for most of my brothers and sisters when I say I feel like we never missed out on anything as kids or teenagers. In fact, we probably had more freedom and fun than a lot of kids. We had imagination that took us everywhere. We were all very close in age; we had a small house with a large front yard with a very big backyard that led to a creek with a big oak tree that fanned out over the creek. A creek and a tree can have more entertainment than you can imagine. We made most of our own fun because my parents instilled great confidence in each one of us to be our own person. They demanded hard work, honesty, and personal responsibility from us. Mom and Dad always helped me to get whatever it was I wanted or needed. Not that I didn't have to work for what I wanted, but if I came up a little short, they were always there, willing to be the backup if what I wanted made sense. I can honestly say I had a very happy life growing up.

CHAPTER 2
A SON'S TRAGIC PAIN

One April morning in 1960, my father was getting ready for work when his father, Walter, came into the house dressed for work. Granddad, as we kids called him, lived in a small house on the property that my father and his brothers built for him behind the family home. We called it "The Shed." Dad asked granddad with surprise why he was up.

"Where are you going so early?"

Granddad replied quickly, "With you to work."

This caught Dad by surprise because just the night before they had discussed work and decided Granddad wasn't going. So Dad told him that he wasn't taking him to work with him today. Granddad was insistent that he was going and begged Dad to take him. Most of the time Granddad would just get up, go, and Dad would always take him. But this morning, Dad said he had an odd feeling about taking him with him. Not wanting to hurt his dad's feelings, he just said it wasn't a good day for him to go. Dad made them a beautiful breakfast of bacon, eggs, toast, and coffee.

While they were eating it, Granddad pleaded again and again with Dad saying, "I won't get in the way, Bob. You said you were only going for half a day."

So ignoring his feelings, Dad thought what the heck; it will be a short day. He gave in and said he would take him with him. My dad and his father had a very close relationship, but neither of them could have predicted what the day had in store for them.

My granddad was in great health; he was seventy-three years old and had only a couple things that were wrong with him; one was his eyesight. Many years before, he had put his own eye out with a pocket knife, so he wore glasses. The other was he had lost some hearing in one ear; otherwise, he was fit, tall, lean, and energetic for his age.

The morning took on a beautiful glow as the sun came up while they drove to work. It was Dad's favorite time of the day.

They had seen many beautiful sunrises together, but this morning, Granddad remarked, "What a beautiful morning it is; so fresh and springtime clean."

The glistening of the morning dew made the day look extra crisp through the windshield. The temperature was mild and the mountains were always a welcome sight to these two men. They felt at home anytime they were in the mountains. While they drove along in the Jeep, their conversation was limited because of the noise of the engine. The ride to work took an hour, so they arrived just before 6:30 a.m. Turning off the engine. Dad noticed there was still a little mist rising from the moisture on the trees as the sun came up higher in the sky. It was a beautiful sight, he thought, like diamonds glistening up, up, and up.

Dad asked Granddad, "Would you like a little fire to stay warm while I get started?"

But Granddad was anxious to get to business and said, "No, I'll be fine. Let's get to work."

My dad told my mother later that he had an uneasy feeling that he couldn't shake, from the time he woke up that morning. When his dad spoke, the feeling intensified inside of him. They both unloaded the tools from the Jeep that Dad would need to cut the trees—the chainsaw, axes, wedges, and a gas can. They walked down a steep grade to the landing where Dad left his gas can. My dad kept his dad close by him, and sat him down a safe distance away from where he was going to fall the trees. Timber falling is one of the most dangerous occupations. Dad knew the dangers so he took extra precautions, especially this morning.

Everything seemed to be going fine when at almost ten o'clock, Granddad said, "I'm tired, Bob. I think I'll go back up the hill to the Jeep."

My Dad said that would be fine and he then explained to Granddad exactly where he was going to fall the next trees.

He said, "I will meet you back at the Jeep as soon as I fall these last snags, and we will have some lunch."

He watched as his father walked away in the direction of the Jeep, which was the opposite direction of the place where he was falling the snags. When Dad had figured his father was a safe distance away, he started the chainsaw and finished his logging. He gathered up his chainsaw, gas, and tools, and headed back up the hill to the Jeep.

Dad was surprised but not alarmed, when he got back to the Jeep and Granddad wasn't there. Knowing how impatient his dad was—dad thought maybe he had taken a walk or something like that. Or maybe he had gone to relieve himself, so Dad lit up a cigarette and waited for him to return. After finishing his cigarette, he begun to wonder and worry where his dad could be and why he hadn't returned yet. His next thought was of horror, and then dread. That odd feeling he had been feeling most of the morning was back. All of a sudden, he felt sick to his stomach; something was telling him that there was something very wrong.

He started calling, "Dad, Dad!"

With no answer, he ran straight back to where he had fallen the last trees. Now overwhelmed with anxiety and adrenalin, that feeling told him that his father was under that tree and was probably dead. Ripping through the bushes, he now approached the fallen tree with apprehension, hoping against all hope that his father wouldn't be there. He climbed through the branches, pulling and pushing his way to see if he could see anything under them. When he almost reached the top of the fallen tree, he stopped momentarily; could he stand this if his dad was under there? Silently, he prayed for strength, looking down he could see part of what looked like his father's shirt beneath the branches. His heart sank. He carefully climbed down to where he could get a better view. It looked as though his father was there and was face down from what Dad could see of his body. He was trying to make sense out of why his father was even in this area. He must have been turned around. Maybe he hadn't seen the tree and had gotten hit from behind. But why was he over here anyway? Dad cursed repeatedly.

Even though he knew in his heart that his father was dead, he still called out "Dad, Dad, please answer me."

He needed to see if there was any reaction at all. He stood above the tree stunned, not knowing which way to turn. He didn't know what he could do to get his father freed from the tree without crushing him more. The shock of this made him unable to think straight. He felt so alone and afraid. Finally, his senses came back to him and he realized he had to get help. Hope began to stir in him; maybe Dad wasn't hurt that bad, was still alive, and just unconscious, he thought. With new hope, he turned around quickly and struggled to climb up the branches of the newly fallen tree. When he finally freed himself from the tangling branches, he ran back up the hill to the Jeep. In desperation, he started the Jeep. Now he had to pull himself together. Was there anyone around who could help him get that tree off his dad? He was working on pure adrenalin now and realized he had to think harder. The picture of his father under the branches kept returning to his mind. Town was too far away to go for help. Finally, he thought of the logging job down the road. Surely there would be someone there to help him. So he put the Jeep in gear and drove unaware, mindlessly a mile or so to the next logging job to see if there was someone who could help him. As the Jeep spun into the landing, he heard chainsaws buzzing in the distance. He got a sense of the direction from where the sound was coming from and leaped out of his Jeep. He ran toward the sound.

As he ran, he hollered repeatedly, "Help, help, help me!"

Through the clearing of trees, he saw a man just putting down his chainsaw. He ran to him. It was a logger who's name was Ralph. The man knew my dad. Most local loggers knew Bob Simonis. Ralph saw the frantic look on Bob's face.

He grabbed him, saying, "What are you saying, Bob? What's the matter?"

With a distraught look on his face, Bob said, "I need you to help me; I have either hurt or killed my dad."

There wasn't time for Ralph to react; Bob was already headed back to the Jeep. Ralph alerted his partner who came running. He briefly explained that Bob had an emergency. Then he told him to go into town for help, which was ten miles away. Ralph went with Bob to check on the situation. As both men drove back to where Dad had left his father, they didn't say much to one another. There was a scary silence between them. Bob smoked another cigarette; Ralph could feel the tension building in Bob as they came closer to the landing. He was afraid to ask Bob any questions. They both jumped out of the Jeep and ran, without taking time to turn off the ignition. Ralph followed close behind Bob as he ran down the steep hill.

Again, a thought went through Bob's mind as he was running. He hoped that his father would be gone from under the tree. Maybe he would be sitting there waiting impatiently for Bob to return. However, as the two men came closer to the fallen tree and scaled down it, Bob could still see part of his father's body exactly as he had left it. Now the realization of the situation was sinking in, and Bob was positive his dad was dead. An hour or more had passed since he had logged the last tree. Ralph desperately fought through the branches of the large tree to get to Walter, but after surveying all the angles, Bob and Ralph agreed it was hopeless. Even if they used their chainsaws to try to free him, the weight of the tree would crush him more. There was nothing more they could do except wait until help arrived. They could tell the tree was clearly on top of Walter and it was too heavy to budge.

"If only I had a piece of equipment," Bob said, "I could free him."

The helplessness of waiting almost killed my dad.

It seemed to take forever for help to get there. While waiting, Dad said that he was glad for the first time in his life that his mother was already dead. Ralph told Bob that he would go back to the landing to wait for help, and then he would show them where Bob was waiting. It wasn't long before Bob saw the sheriff and a deputy appear at the base of the tree. Ralph was with them and showed the sheriff and the medics the way to where Walter's lifeless body laid. The sheriff looked rather perplexed at how he was going to get to where Bob was standing. With caution, they both followed Ralph down through the broken branches of the tree, and then they carefully approached the body. The medic went in front of the sheriff and checked for vital signs in the best way he could. He then looked up and said to the sheriff that he believed Walter Simonis was dead. The sheriff was already radioing for the proper equipment to remove the tree from the body. He also asked that the coroner would be dispatched to the site, too. During the time when Bob was standing there watching, he felt completely powerless to do anything for his father.

When the equipment arrived, it took another hour to free Granddad's body. While that was going on, the coroner questioned him, and took down the information from my father regarding how the accident had happened. Looking over into the now beaten down path, Bob saw the deputies carrying the body bag with his father in it. He watched as they walked past him, up the hill, and loaded it into the coroner's van. When the coroner was through with his questions, he told my dad that his father's body would be at the county morgue, and that he would have to call a funeral home of his choice to pick him up. Ralph had offered to drive Dad home but he wouldn't leave his Jeep or consider feeling that vulnerable. He thanked him but said he would get home just fine. As they all left, he rolled another cigarette, and stood alone alongside his Jeep. He was in shock and disbelief of what had just happened. Meanwhile, that sick, odd feeling now consumed him. He couldn't cry. He just asked himself why; why had he let his dad talk him into going with him this morning?

He loaded his tools into his Jeep and slowly drove to the main road while the image of his father leaving him to go to the Jeep played again and again in this mind.

On his way home, there was a woman on the side of the road with a flat tire. Dad, being the person he was, stopped to change her tire and got her back on the road. He had introduced himself to her as Robert Simonis, but had said nothing about the ordeal he had just gone through. The next day she read in the newspaper about a logging accident, and recognized Bob's name. She brought flowers to the house saying she was so sorry. He never let on that anything was wrong and she was so thankful to have someone help her on that mountain road that she never noticed he was having any problems.

For reasons that seemed unknown at the time, something had told my father that he shouldn't take his father to work with him that morning. Dad said that he felt it and knew it, but for some strange reason, he couldn't tell his father no that morning. He tried but he just wouldn't take no for an answer.

Sometimes I think, subconsciously, we know our own destiny, however tragic the end is. Dad had two brothers and three sisters living at that time. None of them ever blamed Dad for their father's death. I believe, though, that Dad silently carried the guilt of his father's death with him. However, I never heard him say another word about it.

CHAPTER 3

BOB'S INJURY

At the age of fifty-two, my dad was logging in Oroville, California, about seventy miles away from home. He liked to camp during the workweek, and then come home for the weekends in the summer. When work was too far away, it was easier and more restful for him than driving back and forth. It was Friday morning, the end of the week; he went to work as usual that morning. After falling trees all morning, he and his partner, John Bruce, broke for lunch.

While they were eating, Dad said to John, "I'm sure tired today and can't wait for this day to end. I just can't get myself going."

John said, "Here, have some more coffee. That should get you going."

This was surprising to John, because for as long as he had worked with Bob, he hadn't heard this kind of talk out of him; he just wasn't the kind of man to complain about anything. John had seen him with his fingernails black and blue, but you wouldn't hear a whine out of him. Dad loved to tell the little kids that a bear got him whenever he had a new injury. He was usually too tough for his own good.

The afternoon was warm and a little breezy, which made it not too hot for summer; John and Dad took an extra few minutes to enjoy the quietness of nature and to let their lunch settle before they continued working.

Breaking through the silence, Bob said, "Let's get back to work, get this job finished, and go home."

After cutting the first tree and watching it thunder to the ground, Dad started bucking it. Bucking a tree consists of cutting all the limbs off the trunk of the tree and then cutting the tree into measured lengths of logs. This is extremely dangerous work because the branches can be holding the tree in place, and when they are cut, the tree or limbs can break loose moving quickly in any direction. This tree was lying with a lot of the branches twisted. As Dad was bucking it, the pressure on one of the branches as he cut it jumped back with such force that it hit him in the leg. It threw him twenty feet into the air. For a few moments, he didn't know what had happened to him. He laid there not moving, tangled in the branches. He rolled over, tried to get up, but was overcome with excruciating pain and yelled out. John Bruce was a few feet away and saw something out of the corner of his eye. Seeing Bob lying on the ground, he threw his chainsaw and came running over to him. John could see he was hurt badly; his left leg seemed to be laying in the wrong direction. Bob was conscious but he was moaning and rolling.

John yelled at him and bent down to steady his shoulder, "Lay still. I'll get help! I think you broke your leg."

Bob was only able to say, "Don't leave me! Load me in your truck and take me to the hospital."

DEATH MATTERS | 21

John was a big man; he looked the situation over, and then said, "Bob, this is going to hurt like hell for me to pick you up."

There was no one else around that could help him with Bob. He was sure that his leg was broken.

"Okay, let me get my truck closer to you," he said.

John ran to his truck and drove it as close as he could to Bob. Bob was in such pain that John didn't quite know how to get him in the truck without hurting him more.

He said, "Bob, I will pick you up as gently as I can, and I will put you in the bed of the truck."

Bob could only shake his head. John had some clothing, jackets, T-shirts, and so on behind his seat. He grabbed them and threw them in the back for some padding under Bob's leg. This gave him an idea. He got some rope from the back of the truck and told Bob that he was going to wrap his leg before he moved him. There was no reaction from Bob as he was in too much pain. John carefully wrapped a heavy coat around the knee area and lower leg. Then he tied it with the rope. It gave his leg more support than he had anticipated it would. Bob seemed to relax somewhat, or maybe he passed out for a moment. John didn't really know which, so he figured this was the time to pick him up. He loaded him into the truck without much trouble and drove him to the hospital in Oroville. It was only a fifteen-minute drive, but to John, it seemed like forever. Bob just laid his head back and moaned.

Around four in the afternoon, my mother received a call from Oroville Hospital. They said that Mr. Simonis had been injured in a logging accident, and he was going into the operating room. The woman on the phone said his left leg had been broken in several places; the doctor said to repair it would take surgery. Mother asked if it could wait until he could be transferred to Redding, but the woman calling said she was only relaying the message, and she believed the surgery was already in progress.

I was married and living a couple miles away from my parent's home. I had just gotten home from work when the phone rang. It was my mother asking me to drive her down to Oroville.

She only said, "Your dad has been injured and I have to go right now."

I told her I would be right over to get her. On the freeway, Mother was very nervous. She probably smoked ten cigarettes. I tried to take her mind off of Dad's injury by saying maybe it wasn't too bad. We both knew she was worried about Dad, and worried about how this would affect them financially. We got to the hospital and Dad was still in surgery. I got my mother a cup of coffee to calm her nerves; Dad had been hurt logging before but nothing that required hospitalization or surgery. We waited in the waiting room for two hours without a word as to his condition. When the doctor came out to talk to us, he said that Dad's leg had been broken in five different places. He had set his leg and put it into a cast that went up to the top of his thigh. He also said he would keep him in the hospital for a week, and then send him home if everything was all right. He said that he would keep him sedated for most of the night so we might as well go home. Because we weren't prepared to stay overnight, we waited until they put him in a room. After talking to the night nurse, we decided to take the doctor's advice, and we drove back home. The next morning, my sister, Phoebe, and I were at the hospital when he woke up. For several days, we drove back and forth, always leaving one of the family members in the hospital with him until he was released to come home.

The cast that they put on Dad was very cumbersome and his leg was extremely painful. It was a difficult and long ride home. Once at home, it was very hard to try to make dad comfortable. He couldn't lie down, so his bed was out of the question. Mother was thinking about renting a hospital bed when a friend of Dad's offered a reclining chair. That worked perfect, or as good as could be expected. He could recline enough to sleep and his leg was elevated at the same time. Dad was in that chair for nine months. The chair, the time, the injury, and the inability to support his family, all put a tremendous strain on him. He had always been an active person. Now all he could do was sit in a chair. This was such a burden for him to carry day in and day out that the guilt was beginning to overwhelm him. Not being able to care for his family's needs, and also his wife's needs, made him severely depressed. He became a little grumpy and very negative, which all of the family could see by his attitude towards most things. Not that we could blame him. One thing that brought him great enjoyment was the time he got to spend with his youngest daughter, Hester, who was three at the time, and his first granddaughter, Sarah, who was just an infant. He had always worked so much before this accident that this gave him some real one-on-one loving time with the girls. Regardless of his rough exterior, he had a passionate heart, and he was very sensitive to the kids' needs.

When the day finally came to have the cast taken off his leg, he had anticipated that his life would return to normal. But his dreams were shattered when he tried to put his weight on his leg. He was mentally and physically weakened; more than he realized from sitting in a chair for months. His leg had healed great, even though there wasn't any physical therapy to help him regain his strength at that time. After a short time, he tried to resume his normal activities. He was very stubborn. He wouldn't listen to the doctors or his wife about the length of time he needed to be completely healed physically. Mentally he wouldn't allow himself to be defeated. He decided to return to logging. My mother tried to convince him that it was too soon after the accident and that he wasn't ready to return to work. Nevertheless, he wasn't listening and especially if it came from her. He held an emotional resentment toward her that seemed to grow daily. He needed to show her he was still the man he used to be regardless of how he really felt.

A few weeks after the cast was removed, Dad went back to work. It was incredibly hard on him; almost impossible. He complained that his lower back was hurting. He took more breaks than he ever had before. He was starting to realize that it was going to take time and a lot of effort to try to be what he was before this accident. On Friday of his first week back, he could hardly get going that morning. Several times that day he urinated blood. He came home and told Mary. She called the doctor immediately and made an appointment for the next week with a friend of hers who was a urologist. Dad rested most of the weekend and the blood seemed to be much less frequent when he wasn't exerting himself.

My father went to his doctor's appointment by himself on Monday morning. By 2:00 p.m., my mother received a phone call from him. He said that he was in the hospital and that the doctor was running all kinds of tests on him. He had diagnosed him with probable prostate cancer. He said the doctor would operate on him the following morning for a large tumor in his prostate. Dad asked Mother if she would send someone up to get his Jeep and bring it home. He didn't want to leave it overnight in the hospital parking lot. Mother was completely flabbergasted at his calm demeanor on the phone with such a serious situation. Was there something here she was missing? The Jeep seemed more important than his health or a second opinion on his diagnosis.

She said, "Bob, I don't think your Jeep should be your main concern at this time. You need to come home."

She tried to discourage his hasty decision on such a radical surgery.

"What's the rush? You said the doctor hasn't even completed the tests yet," she said. "You need some time to think this over and talk to me. Then we can decide on the appropriate measures to take, Bob. You can't just rush into this."

But Dad wouldn't listen to her. He was adamant that he was going through with the surgery. When he told someone he would do something, he did it, even if it wasn't the right thing for him in this situation. My mother knew she was powerless against his will when he was like this. She knew she needed help to change his mind. She just needed a day or two until she could figure out the best way to approach this possible diagnosis. He wasn't thinking right. The shock of such a serious diagnosis as cancer hadn't really given him time to think. So Mother did the next best thing when Dad acted unreasonable or stubborn. She called me.

I had been expecting a call from Mother to let me know what the doctor had found that was making Dad urinate blood. I figured she would call with the results of his doctor's appointment. The phone rang at my house.

Mother said, "Georgia, your dad just called from the hospital."

"What?" I asked, not even letting her finish her sentence.

"He went to see the doctor this morning, and now he's in the hospital. He says he's going to be operated on in the morning for possible cancer. You have to help me get him out of there and take him to Dr. Yen," she said.

Dr. Yen is a Chinese acupuncturist.

I couldn't believe my ears, and I said, "Mother, do you mean that he has cancer?"

I had never expected to hear this kind of result, and I was shocked. I just thought that maybe his kidneys were giving him some problem. Cancer never crossed my mind.

She said, "That's what he's telling me, but we can't let him be operated on without a second opinion or checking into optional treatments first. I don't know anything about prostate cancer at all. So you need to help me get him out of that hospital today and bring him home so we can discuss it. You know what happens when certain men's influence gets hold of him. He just won't say no to them."

It wasn't that this doctor had some sort of strange influence over my dad; it was just the way Dad reacted to some men's authority.

"I'll be right over," I said to my mother.

I hung up the phone and wondered what other awful thing could happen to Dad. I changed my clothes, grabbed my purse, and left the house.

On the way to the hospital, I asked Mother to explain what was exactly going on with Dad. She said she didn't really know and gave me a brief rundown of her conversation on the phone with him.

She said, "We'll find out more when I speak to the doctor."

I thought this wasn't going to be easy. I would have to stand up to my father and speak to him in a manner I had never done before. I didn't know how I was going to do it. He was a man of his word, and took great pride in it. Leaving the hospital would mean going against what he said that he was going to do. This would be a very difficult thing for him to do, and I knew it.

Arriving at the parking lot of the hospital, I pulled up and parked right next to his little red Jeep. Just seeing that Jeep made me sad for my dad. He had been injured many times, and now he might have cancer. I related the word cancer with death. Was my dad going to die? My eyes clouded up, and I said to myself out loud, "Stop!" I can't let myself think like that right now. I locked the car door, and Mother and I walked into the front lobby of the hospital. At the front desk, I asked for the room number for Mr. Simonis' room. They said he was in room 264-A on the second floor. While riding the elevator up to the second floor, Mother reiterated to me what we had to do. We had to convince Dad to come home!

Mom and I stood in front of the closed door to room 264. Taking a deep breath, I pushed open the door. Dad was alone in the room. The bed next to him was empty—Thank God! I feared this was going to get embarrassing. He was sitting up in bed with a hospital gown on. At first, Mother and I just said hello. I came close and kissed him on the cheek. We didn't want Dad upset right from the start, so Mother just let me take over. I asked him if he was all right.

"What did the doctor say was wrong with you, Dad?"

"He thinks I have cancer, and the "sawbones" is going to cut it out of me in the morning," he said with irritation.

I quickly replied, "No! Dad, please let me take you in the morning to see Dr. Yen. He'll help you, and he won't hurt you. This is too invasive! It will have you incapacitated for a long time, and if it is cancer, it could spread. Please, Dad, get up and come with us. You don't want to do this without another doctor's opinion."

He just said, "No."

He wasn't leaving. I pleaded and pleaded with him. I asked him to put on his clothes and at least come home and think about it for the night. He refused each time I asked. I was trying unsuccessfully I might say, to convince him when a nurse came through the door. She said it wasn't visiting hours and that we would have to leave.

My mother spoke up and said, "We aren't going anywhere; he is."

With a puzzled expression, the nurse looked at us. Then she turned and left the room. She came back into the room a couple minutes later and requested that my mother pick up the phone. She said the doctor wanted to speak to her. Mother left the room to take the call at the nurse's station. I took advantage of this time without Mother in the room to ask Dad once more to leave with us. I knew that her presence was upsetting him. He didn't want her to see him as "weak." His will was strong against me, and he said that he wasn't going anywhere.

At the nurse's station, Mother picked up the telephone, remembering that this doctor was a family friend.

She said to him, "Raul, I'm here to take Bob home. I want you to sign the release papers."

She didn't give him time to answer.

"Why, I wasn't even notified of your test results let alone surgery tomorrow. This is a very drastic thing and I think we need a day or two to digest this. Then we can figure out the appropriate action that we need to take for Bob. What's the hurry anyway?"

The doctor then replied, and acted more like a doctor than a friend.

He said, "Mary, Bob has a tumor about the size of a grapefruit in his prostate. That is what's causing the pain in his back and the blood in his urine. I'm pretty sure it's malignant, and if it isn't removed immediately, he will be dead in two months."

Mother said to him, "I need the time to talk this over with Bob and decide from there what we will do. I don't think a day or two is going to make that much of a difference."

The doctor said, "I haven't the time. I'm leaving for a month's trip to Switzerland the day after the surgery."

This topped the whole conversation off.

My mother was so upset she screamed into the telephone, "Do you mean you think you're going to do this drastic surgery on my husband tomorrow, and then leave your patient for a month in someone else's care? Please, just tell the nurse that Mr. Simonis is leaving so that she doesn't give us any trouble."

"If you take him home now, Mary, I will not be responsible for his death," the doctor said.

With that, Mother handed the phone back to the nurse who was trying to act inconspicuous behind the counter.

Back in room 264, I was still working on my dad. He and I had a little small talk, and then a thought crossed my mind of a time before when I was twelve.

I had heard Dad say to Aunt Juju when she was dying with cancer after having surgery, "If I ever had to face what you have gone through, George, [as he called her] I would never let 'those sawbones' cut me open."

So I repeated that to him, hoping it might do something. Just then, the door swung open, Mother broke through the door yelling, and going on about what the doctor had just said to her. She looked at Dad and demanded that he get up and come with us now.

Well, I will never know if it was my mother's yelling through the hospital, or if it was the recollection of that statement he had made years before, but all of a sudden, Dad jumped out of the bed and started getting dressed. You could have heard a pin drop at that moment. I tried not to look at him out of fear that he might reject this decision he seemed to be making.

Under his breath, he grumbled, "If I leave here now, I will never come back!"

I never said a word nor did my mother. I just helped him get his belongings together. Just then, the nurse came through the door and realized Dad was getting dressed.

She said, "Mr. Simonis cannot leave without the doctor signing a release form."

Mother spoke up and said to her, "Bring me the papers, and I will sign them."

The nurse was frantic, and wailed, "No, you don't understand. He can't leave until the doctor gets here to sign the papers."

Mother just said, "Watch us."

We all got in the elevator together. I could see the nurse rushing towards the telephone while the doors were closing. It was a quiet ride down to the lobby. We walked out of the hospital without saying a word to each other. I felt as though Dad really felt relieved. He might have been embarrassed by the method we used to exit the hospital, but I could see the relief in his face. He would have never admitted it. He was too proud, but it was written all over his face. He walked straight to his Jeep, got in, and drove himself home. I was exhausted from this whole ordeal. I drove my mother home. Dad's Jeep was already there when we drove up. I decided not to go into the house. I figured I had done my job for now; I got him out of that hospital. I was going home to my husband and children. I needed the emotional support from my husband. Tomorrow was going to be another challenging day.

I just let Mother out of the car, and said, "Tell Dad I will be here in the morning to take him to Dr. Yen's."

She agreed with me and gave me that all-knowing look we sometimes had between each other.

PART TWO

Chapter 1
Acupuncture to the Rescue

I awoke early from a restless night full of dreams. In my mind, I went over how I was going to deal with my father this morning. I was somewhat frightened that he might have just decided to be his stubborn self and not do anything for his illness. On the other hand, he might just decide not to let me or any of us help him at all. He might not even be at home for me to take him anywhere. I laid there in my bed imagining all of these different scenarios. It was six o'clock in the morning, too early to leave yet. The doctor's office didn't open until at least nine o'clock. I knew that my dad would be up. He was always an early riser. I waited a short time, and then I picked up the telephone. I called my parent's home.

My little sister, Margaret, answered the phone in a sleepy voice.

"Did I wake you up? It's me, Georgia," I said. "Is Dad awake?"

I didn't wait for her to answer me.

"Will you get up and tell Dad that I will be over in a little while to pick him up, and we'll go to see Dr. Yen?:

She said, "I think he's up and outside. Do you want me to get him?"

I didn't want to speak to him on the telephone, in case he might say he didn't want me to come over.

"No," I said quickly. "Just tell him when he comes in what I said, and don't go back to sleep and forget."

I hung up the phone. I had about two hours to get myself ready and to conjure up the courage I needed to deal with the situation. I had to get my mind ready more than anything else. It was very hard thinking about facing Dad this morning after speaking to him, as I had to do in the hospital yesterday. The emotional aspect seemed overwhelming to me now. I broke down and cried. I hadn't allowed myself to think of losing my father so far. I felt sorry for him, and I felt scared for myself. But I knew that we were doing the right thing at the moment. At least Dr. Yen wouldn't hurt him.

When I drove up to the house, Dad was sitting on the front porch smoking; he looked tired, beaten down. The expression on his face made me feel bad for him. I had never spoken to my father in the manner I did the day before. I pulled into the driveway to park my truck. Dad got up and walked towards me. I held my breath thinking he might tell me he wasn't going with me.

Instead, through my window, he said, "I'm driving my Jeep if you want to go with me."

Happily, I said, "Okay, let me park!"

I finished parking my truck noting that he looked better now than when I drove up. I realized this was very hard on him; yesterday he had been given a death sentence. Still, I was relieved that my earlier fears were uncalled for. I felt better. I jumped in the Jeep and we drove off.

We drove down the freeway not saying much to one another, but that was all right with me. We were on the freeway on our way to Dr. Yen's office. Dad wasn't in the hospital in surgery this morning. My family had seen Dr. Yen for many years, and he was a trusted doctor and friend. Dr. Yen had only a small office in front of his home. Dad parked the Jeep and we walked to the door. Dad opened the door and held it for me to enter. The little bell above the door tinkled a soft chime. The doctor was expecting us because Mother had called and made the appointment yesterday afternoon. She had given Dr. Yen a brief rundown on what Dad would be seeing him for. When we arrived, he showed us right into his office.

Dr. Yen said, "Yes, I have been expecting you, please," as he motioned us to sit down.

We sat down. They did a little small talk between them about family, but because of the doctor's limited English and understanding, it was a little difficult to communicate some things. Dad explained to him all the information that the urologist had found through the tests. He explained the procedure that they wanted to do with him. Dr. Yen listened to all that my father said very carefully. Occasionally, I would speak up and help Dad in making the doctor understand exactly what he was saying. When Dad was finished speaking, Dr. Yen questioned all the information we had told him. It was as if he wanted to make sure he had understood it all. When he was confident that he had all the information correct, he then explained to us how cancer tumors grew, how they reacted to herbs, and how he anticipated this type of tumor would react to his treatment. He then excused himself for a short time. Then he came back with a small white paper cup filled with some dark-looking hot herbs that he had cooked for Dad to drink.

He said, "You drink, while we talk."

Slowly, he explained that he would cook and bottle two quarts of a concoction of herbs each week that would help to reduce the tumor. In a couple of months, the tumor should hopefully be reduced in size. In his estimation, if the urologist said he had a tumor the size of a grapefruit, it should be about the size of a lemon by then. It would reduce more as time went on. Each time Dad took a drink, I could see him cringe, yet he was trying not to show it. Dr. Yen went on to say after two months he would request that Dad return to the urologist to have another x-ray taken to confirm the decrease in the tumor's size. I felt so much better, and I could see the relief in Dad. Dr. Yen's attitude was so positive and non-invasive that it gave us both such a feeling of hope for his life. The doctor excused himself again. After a short while, he returned with the two hot bottled herbs. He placed them in brown paper bags and said he would see us next week when he would work on Dad's body after the herbs had a chance to start their job. In addition, he said if we needed anything that we shouldn't hesitate to call him. We thanked him and left the office.

I could tell by Dad's demeanor that he was feeling much better about his health and future. He had confidence in Dr. Yen. He had seen for himself how his herbs and acupuncture had helped many family and friends before. As we left the office, Dad's whole attitude was different. He even talked to me all the way home.

Dad continued to go each week to visit Dr. Yen. Acupuncture originally started in China. It's a method of using very small needles. They're placed under the skin to increase the flow of energy, and are applied to the afflicted area that may be causing a disorder. Dr. Yen used a needleless acupuncture technique. With only his fingers, he would work on what he called the pressure points, mostly in my dad's back. Dad said after the treatments that he always felt energized.

In an amazingly short time, my father's bleeding had stopped. He began to look better; his strength slowly began to return. He noticed that his energy levels had become higher, and he could tolerate much more in his life now. This impressed him so much that he never let himself run out of herbs. If his supply got low before the week was up, he was driving down the freeway in that little Jeep to see the doctor.

Dad was still trying to resume his livelihood of logging, but he had to face the fact that those days were over for him. Even though he felt almost normal again, he didn't have the strength he once had for logging. This was extremely hard for him to accept. He still had several children under the age of eighteen at home that needed him for support. Eventually, he was forced to go on social security. He sometimes took jobs for private individuals over the years that allowed him to help his family. Yes, I said years. Remember, the urologist said he had only two months to live.

CHAPTER 2

THE PROPERTY

It was 1973 when my brother, Si, bought a piece of property with timber and a beautiful natural spring in the mountains of Northern California. His enthusiasm for these fifty-six acres was incredible for a twenty-four-year-old young man. I remember when he took Phoebe and me to see it. He ran from one corner of the property to the next like a maniac. We had quite a time keeping up with him and his excitement for his beautiful new property. Even today, whoever comes there to visit, he shows the same enthusiasm. It had so much potential. His vision of the property becoming his family's home and more was beyond his years.

Dad began going up to this property and helped Si develop it. He spent more and more of his time on this land. He was proud of Si and it brought him great pleasure to get to work with his oldest son. They started by putting a huge army tent up for any of the family that wanted to come up and stay, usually during the weekends. This was just a bare piece of land with tremendous potential that would take a lot of loving care to become something special. Nevertheless, they were both willing to do it along with help from family. They worked many hours a day piping water from the spring to the camp where the tent was. They even piped it into the fire so there would be hot water whenever they wanted a shower as long as a fire was burning. I remember one night the pipe was in the fire and no one was using the hot water. All of a sudden the pipe blew apart like a bomb, and hot water was spurting everywhere. It scared us to death at the time, but we got a good laugh out of it. The whole family spent most of their spare time the first summer camping there on weekends. Mother would bring the kids up and we'd all spend time with Dad. The good times we shared with family and friends were undeniably important to the unity of my family. We had no luxuries up there, but it never stopped us from coming because Dad was staying there. We loved him and knew he loved us. I have always been grateful for the generosity that Si and his wife, Melinda, gave the family. Throughout that summer, Dad seemed to get stronger and happier. Working and seeing his productivity was one of the best remedies for him. By the next spring, Si bought a thirty-five foot travel trailer. He put it up there for Dad to stay in. He and Dad built an addition on the side of the trailer. It was a wonderful room off the side of the kitchen. It had a large wood-burning stove and windows on all three sides that made the trailer warm and cozy. From inside, you could see the tall trees, hear the wind whisper through them, and at times, you could hear the wind thunder. The creek that flowed behind the yard gave a sense of tranquility to all. With all the work that was going on at the property, Dad chose to stay up in the mountains most of the time at the property. We actually called it, "The Property." The environment of "The Property" was extremely conducive to the welfare of Dad's health. He could rest when he wanted. He could work when he wanted. He ate good, and most of all, there was that naturally pure spring water for him to drink. Dr. Yen told him how important pure water was to him. He also didn't have the stress of the everyday family, which was an added benefit for his health. He missed his wife enormously, but because of the prostate cancer, he had become impotent. It became increasingly more difficult for him to be around her. He still loved her very much, but he couldn't allow his emotions for her to interfere with his progress of healing. He decided it was much easier and wiser for his health to live in the mountains. During the years that he spent at "The Property," there weren't more than a couple days in a row that he didn't drive that little red Jeep down the hill to the family house to see us kids. Mother also drove up the hill to be with him. Our family unity and responsibility to each other remained strong. It wasn't as if Mom and Dad were separated. The kids that were still at home understood that Dad was sick and needed to stay in the mountains. We knew we were all happiest when some of us were around him.

At one time, Si and his wife lived there in a trailer. My husband and I bought a trailer and moved up there, too. Then Phoebe and her husband did the same. We had quite a community that winter and a lot of fun.

Time went along and my thought of Dad being sick didn't register much at all anymore. He didn't look or act as if he was sick. Yet, after the first year or so, I noticed that he wasn't drinking his herbs as steady as he did before. He was so active and looked so good that I don't think anyone would have noticed he was sick at all. One day when I had spent many hours with him, I brought up the fact that he hadn't been drinking his herbs.

I asked him, "Are you out of herbs or have you stopped taking them?"

His reply was, "I'm tired of that bug juice. I think I'll just stop for awhile."

The doctor had suggested he stop smoking, drinking coffee, and working so hard. The doctor hadn't suggested that he stop taking his herbs. If he had followed just one of those suggestions, maybe he would have lived longer than he did. Instead of following the doctor's orders, I noticed he began taking on extra private work, like falling trees, building ponds, running heavy equipment, and whatever people asked of him. He wasn't just attracted by the money. It mattered to him and gave him satisfaction that he was being useful. When he wasn't doing hard labor, he grew garden vegetables, planted fruit trees, picked berries, milked cows, and fed chickens, all for his family. He achieved so many wonderful things up there. He milked a cow named Maybelle, which he cursed, twice a day for two years. My brother Jocko brought it to him. Dad prepared the milk for the family.

My two small boys, Robert, [named after Dad] Kenneth, and I spent many wonderful times with Dad at that property. We went for many walks together and he enjoyed watching the kids swim in the pond that he and Si had built. He would let them ride on the bulldozer with him. He did all the things a granddad should to show his love for them. I knew this land was good for him. He told me once that this land was what sustained him; it gave him a reason to go on, to be useful, and to have a purpose for his life other than being sick. That was good enough for me. I couldn't argue with that. Therefore, I couldn't find it in my heart to say anything to him about his herbs.

About a year after he stopped taking the herbs, the old symptoms started to return. The pain in his back was worse, and he began to feel weak again. But he didn't let on to anyone. When the blood in his urine returned, it scared him enough that he went straight back to the Chinese doctor. He began the same treatment all over again. Dr. Yen never scolded him for his inconsistencies in taking the herbs, but he did say that consistence was the key to controlling and curing his condition. The expense for Dr. Yen's services was not the issue with Dad when he decided to discontinue the herbs. He would just get feeling so good that he thought he could do without them. Dr. Yen was more interested in healing Dad than the monetary part of his treatment and care. He was following in his own father's footsteps to find the right cure for each type of cancer. Money wasn't what his treatment of Dad was about.

The herbs seemed to work faster this time. Soon, the bleeding was under control again, and he started feeling better almost immediately.

Years went by. I have both happy and sad memories of those times. Life was pretty much just life, kids growing up, finishing school, getting married and so on. Many times my father gave up drinking the herbs only to start them again when his condition demanded it. He never took them on a regular schedule like he had in the beginning. After about seven years of taking them, he stopped them altogether. He was getting tired of them and all the battles he was fighting. It took almost a year for us to notice the visible signs of his declining health. He was becoming too weak to take good care of himself like he always had. At the same time, he was his own worst enemy. He wouldn't accept help or advice from anyone in the family. He seemed hell-bent on doing everything the hard way. His teeth began to loosen; he even pulled one out himself. When he told Mother about them, she tried to get him to see a dentist. It took a month of terrible pain before he gave in and agreed to see a dentist.

CHAPTER 3

GIVING BACK

In the early spring of 1980, my dad's teeth became so bad that the dentist said they were poisoning his system, and he would have to have them all removed. He had given up a lot of his battles now with his own stubbornness, but he gave in and had his teeth pulled out. He stayed at the house more with his wife and the family. He hadn't the strength anymore to work or drive that little Jeep up and down the hill. He was glad to be home, and he was glad to have us all taking care of him. His health seemed to be declining rapidly. He had always carried the same weight throughout his life even through the years of his illness. However, he was now becoming noticeably thinner. I could tell he was in pain just by the way he walked, but he still didn't complain about it.

By September, his health was really failing, and he couldn't ignore it anymore. He came to my house and stayed for ten days with my husband, Kim, me, and our three children. At the time, my mother was taking some of the younger kids to a swim meet. She also needed a little time away from all the pressure of his illness.

I asked him, "Please come and stay with me, Dad. Mother will be back in a week and I will take care of you while she's gone."

"No, I don't need to intrude in your life," he said.

I knew he couldn't be left alone and it would have made my mother so nervous to leave him home that she wouldn't have been able to enjoy any part of the trip.

So I just said, "Dad, I insist. We want to spend the time with you. I will take care of you and the grandkids will love having you here."

When he finally agreed, we packed up his stuff and loaded him into my truck. We had a small house so we gave him our bedroom so that he could feel a little more comfortable. However, I soon discovered there wasn't much I could do to help him feel comfortable.

He was in more pain than I had imagined. He had kept his pain hidden from all of us. He needed a doctor's care now. Each night I slept in the next room, and I would wake up hearing him moaning in pain. I went to the door and listened. I felt so helpless. What could I do to help him? All I could think about was that he must see a doctor. He couldn't continue to suffer from the pain like that without some relief.

Many times, I asked him, "Dad, is there anything I can do to help you? What can we do for that pain?"

He would just kind of brush me off saying, "I'm all right. Go back to bed."

I decided to talk to my sisters about the pain he was in. We made plans to take him to a holistic doctor we knew in Oregon state. It was a long trip for a sick man in pain, but we knew that this doctor would help his pain. He had treated Dad for other ailments off and on. While my sister made the arrangements, I told Dad what we wanted to do. I expected objections from him, but he had none. He was at the point that any help would have been welcomed if it gave him some relief from the pain he was having.

He had been watching a miniseries on television called "Shogan." Each evening when it was on, he would get in my recliner and watch the complete two-hour series without missing a minute of it. He actually enjoyed it. We held off on the trip to Oregon until the movie was over because he was so captivated by it. I was so blessed to have had that time to spend with my father in my home.

Mary and Phoebe rented a van, and we put a bed in the back so that Dad could be somewhat comfortable. Then they drove him to the holistic clinic in Oregon. They stayed with him in the clinic for a week. The doctor ran every kind of test necessary to see if anything could be done to help him. At the conclusion of the tests, the doctor sat down with all three of them. He explained the problems and the measures that had to be taken as honestly as he could and with great compassion.

He began with, "Bob, to start with, you are in very poor health. This is not good news. I don't know how long you can live in this condition. You have a lot of different things going on in your body. I will do anything in my power to help you as much as I can. I have some medications that will help you with pain, and we will start with that first. I think that will give you some relief," he said.

"First of all, only one of your kidneys is working, and not well at that. Your heart is damaged and only about half of it is working. That's why your feet and legs are swollen. It's harder for the heart to pump enough blood to your extremities with the damage it has. Your liver is toxic, and it's failing to do its job. I suspect the cancer has damaged these organs. I don't know if there is anything I can do to help you with the cancer, except give you the pain medication at this time. These are your vital organs, and you know as well as I do, Bob, if they aren't working properly, you're in immediate danger of losing your life. One or all of them could give out at any time on you. I suggest you go home when we are through here and see your family doctor. I think you should be hospitalized. You should be on oxygen so you will be able to breathe better, and your body needs more oxygen. Emphysema is making your lungs work too hard. The oxygen will help the other organs also," he said.

Dad just sat there without saying a word for some time.

Then he turned to the doctor and said, "I think by the way I feel, I knew most of that. I want to thank you for your honesty and for all the help you are trying to give me."

My sister, Phoebe, said she was trying to control her emotions; she was ready to burst out crying, run out of the room, and scream. Both of my sisters knew now, like I did, the bad condition Dad was in. That's why we had to take him there. Hearing all the things that were wrong with him from the doctor made them realize that Dad didn't have too much time left to live.

The doctor gave Dad medication, and the next day they all drove back home. Dad tolerated the ride much better going home. Maybe it was the medication, and maybe it was having an answer to what was progressively happening to him. I believe he didn't have to be told that he didn't have much time to live; he had known it for sometime. However, having it confirmed in front of some of the family took the burden out of what he had been carrying by himself. He didn't have to be so tough now.

When the girls and Dad got back home, Mother was home, too. They had kept me posted daily on Dad's condition while they were gone so I had kept Mother informed, too. She knew everything that we knew. The knowledge that the man she had loved for thirty-three years was dying. It was more than upsetting to her, but she kept her emotions to herself. She didn't openly cry in front of us kids. I can remember only one time when I saw my mother crying. She was overwhelmed with the behaviors of some of us older kids, and Dad was not helping support her in disciplining us. She started screaming at him that she needed his help and support. Then she picked up a bowl of floating candles that were on the table and threw them across the room. She covered her eyes, cried, and ran into the bathroom. She didn't come out for an hour. We all just looked at each other and didn't say a word. Mother was always yelling about something with thirteen kids to raise, but her reaction this time was something we had never seen from her. She was very strong, but it wasn't until I had children of my own that I understood her frustration that day.

She stayed by Dad's side, trying to be strong for both of them and all of us kids. The whole family took turns caring for Dad around the clock. We never left him alone. One afternoon I came in when my brother was helping Dad to the bathroom. When they came out, I could see that my dad was very weak and agitated. We had been trying to get him to go to the hospital for the past week. He needed more medical help than we could give him at this point. For Dad, going to the hospital was declaring defeat; it was surrendering to the disease that had ravaged his spirit and his body for so long. I came to him as Si helped him down on the bed.

I gently said, "Dad, what can I do to help you?"

He looked at me with the most pitiful look I will never forget.

He said, "I can't piss! Do you know what happens if you can't piss?"

I said, "Yes, Dad, I do. You have to go to the hospital. It will be all right."

Chapter 4

The Hospital

While I was in the bedroom with Dad and Si, Mother had gone to the phone and called our family doctor. She had met him twenty-four years earlier when he was the only doctor who would come to the hospital to help her deliver her sixth baby. He was three months premature and she had a difficult birth. Her doctor had refused to come when he was called to the early birth. Dr. Jantzen was a godsend to Mother at the time. The baby, my brother, Jocko, was a miracle child. He weighed in at two pounds, fourteen ounces. He grew to become the largest adult in the family and the one with the biggest mouth. Mother had been keeping the doctor up to date on Dad's condition, and he knew it was only a matter of time before he had to admit Mr. Simonis to the hospital.

The phone rang three times.

"Hello, Dr. Jantzen here!"

"Hello doctor, this is Mary Simonis. I'm calling about Bob. I think we have somewhat of an emergency today. He hasn't urinated, and he says he needs to, but he can't. He's very weak."

"I'll meet you at the hospital. It sounds like we might have to admit him," he said.

Dr. Jantzen's demeanor was always calm.

There was a lot of confusion in the house after Mother told the boys [who were all trying to help] that the doctor was expecting Dad at the hospital. I felt a sense of relief, but I was also afraid. Si was holding on to Dad to support him through the house and out the door, when my Grandmother Nanny came out of her room and stopped them.

With the most worried look I have ever seen on her face, and with tears in her eyes, she said, "Don't worry, Bob, you'll be all right."

She kissed and hugged him wondering if she would ever see him alive again. She always held Dad with a high respect and truly loved her son-in-law. I couldn't hold back my tears. In fact, we all had tears in our eyes as we watched our father leave the house, not knowing if he would ever return home alive again.

Dr. Jantzen was waiting at the hospital when we arrived. Dad seemed to be getting worse by the minute, so the doctor immediately admitted him. The doctor listed his condition as critical, and in the last stages of pulmonary emphysema with carcinoma of the bladder. His orders were only to make Mr. Simonis as comfortable as possible. He told my mother that Bob could die at any time. The only physical procedure he ordered was to insert a catheter to help Dad urinate. Then he ordered some mild pain medication [my dad hadn't been in as much pain now]. He also left an order that one or more family member would be helping with Mr. Simonis at all times.

The family maintained a constant twenty-four-hour vigil at his bedside. We had taken care of him for so long that we couldn't turn over our responsibility of him now. There is research now that proves that ill patients do better with their families around them. However, at that time, the nursing staff didn't quite know how to handle us in their territory. There were designated visiting hour times usually two hours, two times a day at most hospitals, and that was the only time the hospital staff wanted outside people there.

After a day or two, the nurses adjusted very well to the family being there. We brought in all of Dad's food and fresh spring water daily. We fed him, and we bathed him. Once or twice every shift, a nurse would look in on us and ask if we needed anything. They were very helpful to us.

One nurse said, "I wish all the families would stay and help with our patients. It sure would make our jobs easier."

We were very grateful to Dr. Jantzen and the hospital staff for allowing us that freedom.

My dad was in a dying state and we all knew it. He was in and out of consciousness most of the ten days he was at the hospital. The doctor said he only had a short time to live, and he was amazed that he was still alive every time he came to see him. Some of the time Dad was completely coherent, but other times he would talk about his younger days as if it was happening right then.

I was caring for him one day when all of a sudden he looked up and said, "George, go down there and tell Hank to get my gas can. Go down the hill!" he yelled.

Realizing he was hallucinating or something, I said, "Okay."

Well, that wasn't good enough. He became agitated and insisted that I go down the hill. So I acted it out and went to the end of the bed, stood there a moment, and then came back up by him. He settled right down and went back to picking at the air, like there was something there.

When the grandkids would be in the room, he would say, "Don't let those little bastards get in those spider webs. They will get all over them." [Little bastards was a pet name he used].

Maybe it was the medication, but he would pick at his blankets and his clothes like he was picking spider webs off of something, and then he would toss them to the wind. It wasn't as though he was picking his skin as some medications make the nerves irritated. He did it most of the time that he was in the hospital.

Another time I had just started to walk away from the bed when out of the blue Dad said, "My mom was just here."

I was really surprised and interested in his statement, but didn't want to let on, so I said, "She was?"

"Yes," he said. "Didn't you see her?" [His mother died in 1951.]

I said, "No, what did she say?"

He replied as normal as ever, "Nothing, she just came to see me. She comes all the time."

I tried to pry more information from him about his mom, but that was all he had to say. Knowing my dad, he would never make a story up like that unless he had actually seen her. My own belief is that when he was in and out of consciousness, close to death, his spirit or soul was experiencing both worlds. He would see his mother who was waiting for him to cross over into the spirit world. Before we had taken him to the hospital, he had told me and other family members about a little creature in the corner of the bedroom ceiling that he was seeing.

He pointed to one corner and said, "Do you see that little bastard up there? He's good. He tries to protect me, but you see that bastard over there?" as he pointed to the other corner. "He wants me, and he's trying to get me!"

I agreed with him and watched as he kept checking the corners. Whatever was there that he was seeing, I can only guess, so I just let it go.

After a little more than a week in the hospital, Dad seemed to rally and kept asking to go home. He was now conscious most of the time, was eating well, and wasn't in pain. He wanted Mother around him as much as possible. He would ask for her if he couldn't see her. One time she was asleep in the hospital bed next to him when he asked for her. I showed him she was there, and he looked at her and fell right back to sleep. She was at the hospital as much as possible. I was excited that it seemed like Dad was getting better now. I found out that I was extremely naive to think that he was. It has been my experience that terminally ill people appear to be getting better a short time before their last decline. But at the time, I thought he was improving. Dr. Jantzen said that they had done all that the hospital could do for him. He was urinating on his own and was on very low medication that we could administer to him at home. Therefore, he discharged Dad and ordered a home care nurse to come to the house and check on him daily.

CHAPTER 5
THE HOMECOMING

Si pulled his car up to the front walk of my parent's home. The concrete walkway went from the edge of the street to the front porch of the house. My parents had lived in this house for twenty-four years. It was a breezy early fall afternoon. The neighborhood was quiet. A couple of the closest neighbors knew Dad's condition, but since we had lived there that long, our family more or less kept our personal business to ourselves. Some of the neighborhood kids the same age as some of us kids were friends with us. Mother always had us in swimming lessons or private activities that didn't involve the neighbor kids, so school was our only connection to each other. We never had much time for play at home, since there were so many people in the family that there was always work to be done. I was standing at the front window looking out as Si parked the car. He got out and came around to the passenger side. He opened the door and took a wheelchair out of the back seat. This surprised me, because I guess, I was expecting Dad to get out of the car and walk up to the house. When I think back on it, I really was in some sort of denial about Dad's condition.

Si almost had to lift Dad out of the car and into the wheelchair. I was so happy to see him coming home, but in that moment, I realized again that this once vibrant man, my dad, looked very old, weak, and almost helpless. He was home now, but for how long I didn't know. I wonder how sometimes the body is so strong, and other times it's so fragile. I wondered also, why he had to suffer so much. I still look for the answer to that question. As for my dad's suffering, out of his last couple weeks of life, he became a changed man. I noticed there was a difference in the things he said and the way he said them. He was able to openly express himself with a loving-kindness toward each and every one of us kids, and our mother.

He even said one day, "I don't know why I never said that I loved you kids more. I love you all very much."

That was an extremely personal statement for Dad to make, and it meant so much to all of us. Speaking for myself, I knew in my heart that Dad loved us kids. He just wasn't the kind of man that showed his affection in a verbal way. I am thankful that he got past his problems with showing affection and could feel comfortable expressing his feelings to us. It was important to the family and so important for him not to carry that over to deal with possibly in his next life. I believe he resolved many personal issues of this lifetime in that precious time before his death.

My mother's sister, Cody, who was very fond of Dad, came home from a visit to see her daughter in Virginia to help with him after she heard he was so gravely ill.

She always said, "Bob had a wonderful charm about him. He was a truly good, honest man."

Si hadn't left Dad's side in the last couple weeks for more than a few hours. He lovingly put Dad in what we called the boy's bedroom. It was in the middle of the house and was set up so that it was more accessible to what we needed for his care than his own bedroom. Frankly, I know Mother didn't want him to die in their bedroom and leave her with that memory for the rest of the time she lived in that house. She never used her bedroom much after he had been sick in there. Most of the time, she slept in the living room.

The following afternoon after Dad had been released from the hospital, the home care nurse came to the house to check on him. My Aunt Cody had arrived from Virginia and was also staying at the house to help when some of us couldn't be there. She was a vital part in Dad's care, and she usually dealt with the nurse; kept a record of his condition and instructions advised by the nurse. She was also a necessary security for Mother. Mother had two younger sisters that she had raised since her own mother fell short on the job; Aunt Juju, who passed away many years before, and Cody, so they were very close. At certain times through this ordeal, I don't know if Mother would have held up as well as she did without the help and support of Cody. My grandmother Nanny lived at the house with us most of our lives, but she didn't have the same comforting connection with Mother. Nanny was in the room next to Dad's when we brought him home. She was so happy to have him home and amazed he was alive. A few times, she went into his room late at night and read to him to comfort him.

All of our family came and went everyday. We more or less spent most of our time in the bedroom with Dad. Sometimes he was asleep, but if everyone left the room, he would immediately wake up and call for us. He enjoyed the grandchildren and Hester being with him. He would motion them to come up on the bed and talk to him. Sometimes they would draw him pictures, and he would listen intently as they told him what the pictures were about. He never tired of their attention, and he seemed to be revitalized by their young spirits.

I went about my daily activities in the afternoons after my children got out of school. I usually took the morning shift to care for Dad. Mother, Nanny, Cody and some of the younger sisters, who didn't have their own families, shared the evenings and night shifts. Mother, Nanny, and Cody were night owls and never went to bed until the early morning hours anyhow, so one of them would stay awake until I would come to relieve them. My brother-in-law, Mike, who was an LVN nurse at the time, was with Dad a lot in those last days. He was a blessing for all of us. He was such a calm and gentle presence for Dad. Of course, the brothers, Si, Jocko, Henry, and Sam, hardly ever took time to go home; they were at Dad's side most of the time.

The day before Dad passed away, Thursday, October 23, my sister, Sookie, and I were doing a stained glass project in the carport. Dad had been home from the hospital about a week now. A car pulled up and it was the nurse. She came through the carport speaking to us on her way in to check on Dad. She commented on the glass we were cutting. We were working on the project to occupy our time, while still being close if we were needed for anything. Dad was semi-conscious that day; the nurse was only there to check his vital signs and to see if his pain was being managed well. Dad hardly stirred as she checked on him.

When she came out to the living room, she said, "He is much weaker than yesterday, and his vitals are very slow. I'm sorry to say I don't think he will live through the night."

She had said something to the same affect the day before, but today I was able to see the difference in his awareness.

"I'll have Mike stay here tonight," Mother said to her, "just in case we need him."

I still didn't want to let myself believe he was really dying. So about dark, I went in and looked at him sleeping peacefully with several of the family members in the room with him. I wanted to kiss his cheek but didn't want to disturb him. I took my three kids and went home. Even with the children's evening activities diverting my attention off my dad, in the back of my mind, he never left my thoughts. I called at eleven o'clock before I went to bed to check on him and to see if I should come back over. My sister, Nellie, answered the telephone, and said he had eaten some broth earlier but seemed about the same. She said there was plenty of help there tonight, and if anything happened, she would call me. When I hung up the phone, I convinced myself that maybe the nurse was mistaken again and I went to bed.

At one o'clock in the morning, the phone rang. I was disoriented, because I had finally fallen to sleep and couldn't find the phone. I jumped out of bed and almost ran over my husband who was trying to answer it, too. I was praying this wasn't the call I had been expecting. After dropping the phone when he gave it to me, I answered it out of breath. It was my sister, Nellie; she was calling to tell me Dad had just died! I started crying, and I told my husband what he already knew.

He said he would drive me over to the house, but I said, "No, I'll go. Just watch the kids for me until I return."

I threw on some clothes, picked up my baby, and left to the house.

Driving over to the house seemed like I was in a fog. There were very few cars on the streets, and it made me feel alone and a little frightened. I also had a very selfish feeling and felt sorry for myself. I wanted to be there for Dad, for Mother, and for myself when he died.

I said out loud, "I'm sorry, Dad, that I wasn't there with you. Why didn't you wait for me? I'm glad you weren't alone. I hope that like you told me earlier, your mother was there to meet you."

I was weeping so hard I could hardly make out my own words let alone drive. I had been so close to my father that I felt it was my duty to be with him at that time. Now I know in my heart that everything has its time and reasons. I wasn't supposed to be with him at that time. It took me a long time of mentally blaming myself for not being there to come to that realization.

The house was very quiet when I got there. There was no commotion as there had been for so many days. As I came through the laundry room door, I saw my mother in the kitchen just standing by the sink. I went to her, put my arms around her, and wept. I needed her comforting arms at that moment.

She said, "He was just talking to us ten minutes before he took his last breath; Mike tried to revive him with CPR, but to no avail."

"I know, Mother," I said, wrapped in her arms.

Mother was visibly upset, but she wasn't outwardly crying. I went down the hall; I could see most of my sisters and brothers were there in the room surrounding Dad's bed. We were all crying with Dad lying there dead on the bed. He looked like some old man I hardly knew.

I went to the side of the bed, touched his hand, and said quietly, "I love you, Dad."

I think together we said the Lord's Prayer around the bed holding each other. No one knew what to do for a few minutes while we just looked at him, but then like the team we are, we sprung into action. The boys carefully straightened his body and fixed him on the bed, so that he looked like he was asleep. There were phone calls still to be made to some of the family that were not there yet, as all of us wanted to be called if he passed in the night. As a family, we needed to pray together and say our personal good-byes to Dad before we called the doctor.

Dr. Jantzen had left town for the week, but in the anticipation of Mr. Simonis' death, he had informed his on-call doctor, Dr. Ryalls, of Mr. Simonis' condition and that his death was expected. In the event that my dad died while he was out of town, he had instructed us to call Dr. Ryalls. We presumed that he would come to the house to check and pronounce Dad dead as Dr. Jantzen had always come. When someone dies, you must have a doctor or someone of an official capacity to pronounce a death, and then they would be the official signer of the death certificate. Therefore, as we understood that it was standard procedure, Dr. Ryalls would be responsible for signing the death certificate. Then he would report it to the coroner's office, and the coroner's office would send a death certificate to Dr. Ryalls' office for his signature the following morning.

Aunt Cody asked Mother if she wanted her to make the call to the doctor. Cody had worked on his answering service for many years and knew Dr. Ryalls quite well.

Mother said, "Yes."

She seemed relieved that this task didn't fall upon her shoulders right now. It was almost two o'clock in the morning. Cody dialed Dr. Ryalls' numbers and was surprised that the doctor answered the telephone himself. She was expecting the answering service at this time in the morning.

"Hello, this is Dr. Ryalls."

She identified herself and then said, "I'm sorry to wake you, doctor. I'm calling for Mr. Simonis who is my brother-in-law. He died about a half hour ago, and Dr. Jantzen said we were to call you if that happened while he was out of town."

The doctor cleared his throat, and said, "That's okay, Cody. Are Mr. Simonis' eyes fixed open and staring up?"

She thought this was an odd thing to ask her, but she replied, "Yes, they are."

"Then he is dead! You need to call the coroner's office; they will come out and pronounce him dead. You won't need both of us out there this early in the morning."

Cody was at a loss for words. She had learned a long time ago through her job that you didn't question a doctor's authority when he said to do something, even though it was something completely different from what we had been expecting to happen. She told the doctor that's what she would do. She hung up the phone and told Mother that Dr. Ryalls said she was to call the coroner's office to report the death. She said that it didn't seem like the right way to handle this. She had taken many calls of this same nature on her graveyard shift at the answering service, and in a case like this where a person had been hospitalized, and death was expected, it usually never involved the coroner. Following the doctor's instruction, she made the call to the coroner's office. That was the beginning of our nightmare!

Robert Simonis in his U.S. Navy Blues – 1946

Mary Simonis at age 24

Close-up of handcrafted caskets

*L. To R. Margaret, Elizabeth, Sam, Jocko, Poni, Mary, Sookie, Si,
Henry; seated, Phoebe, Hester, Georgia, and Nellie – 1968*

Author GEORGIA SIMONIS at family gravesite

Caskets in family home before their funeral September 2001

Mary Simonis' funeral at Si's family home – 1995

COUNTY OF SHASTA
REDDING, CALIFORNIA

CERTIFICATE OF DEATH
STATE OF CALIFORNIA

4500 1009

PAGE 107

LOCAL REGISTRATION DISTRICT AND CERTIFICATE NUMBER

	1A. NAME OF DECEDENT—FIRST	1B. MIDDLE	1C. LAST	2A. DATE OF DEATH (MONTH, DAY, YEAR)	2B. HOUR
DECEDENT PERSONAL DATA	ROBERT	WINDSOR	SIMONIS	OCT. 24, 1980	0100
	3. SEX	4. RACE	5. ETHNICITY	6. DATE OF BIRTH	7. AGE
	Male	White	American	Jan. 27, 1918	62
	8. BIRTHPLACE OF DECEDENT	9. NAME AND BIRTHPLACE OF FATHER		10. BIRTH NAME AND BIRTHPLACE OF MOTHER	
	Pablo, Mont.	Walter Henry Simonis- Wyo.		Nellie Lou Windsor- Ark.	
	11. CITIZEN OF WHAT COUNTRY	12. SOCIAL SECURITY NUMBER	13. MARITAL STATUS	14. NAME OF SURVIVING SPOUSE	
	U. S. A. (Vet)		Married	Mary Waite-Kent.	
	15. PRIMARY OCCUPATION	16. NUMBER OF YEARS THIS OCCUPATION	17. EMPLOYER	18. KIND OF INDUSTRY OR BUSINESS	
	Dis. Timber Faller	25	— —	Logging- Lumber	
USUAL RESIDENCE	19A. USUAL RESIDENCE—STREET ADDRESS		19B.	19C. CITY OR TOWN	
	3041 Lawrence Road			Redding	
	19D. COUNTY		19E. STATE	20. NAME AND ADDRESS OF INFORMANT—RELATIONSHIP	
	Shasta		California	Walter L. Simonis-Son	
PLACE OF DEATH	21A. PLACE OF DEATH		21B. COUNTY	Rt. 1, Box 146	
	In his own residence		Shasta	Oak Run, Calif. 96069	
	21C. STREET ADDRESS		21D. CITY OR TOWN		
	3041 Lawrence Rd		Redding		

CAUSE OF DEATH	22. DEATH WAS CAUSED BY: (ENTER ONLY ONE CAUSE PER LINE FOR A, B AND C)			
	IMMEDIATE CAUSE (A)	Carcinoma of the Bladder	8 yrs	APPROX. INTERVAL BETWEEN ONSET AND DEATH
	CONDITIONS, IF ANY, WHICH GIVE RISE TO THE IMMEDIATE CAUSE (B)			24. WAS OPERATION PERFORMED — Yes
	STATING THE UNDERLYING CAUSE LAST (C)			26. WAS AUTOPSY PERFORMED — No

	23. OTHER CONDITIONS CONTRIBUTING BUT NOT RELATED TO THE IMMEDIATE CAUSE OF DEATH	27. WAS OPERATION PERFORMED FOR ANY CONDITION IN ITEMS 22 OR 23? TYPE OF OPERATION	DATE
	Pulmonary emphysema	No	

PHYSICIAN'S CERTIFICATION	28A. I CERTIFY THAT DEATH OCCURRED AT THE HOUR, DATE AND PLACE STATED FROM THE CAUSES STATED	28C. DATE SIGNED	28D. PHYSICIAN'S LICENSE NUMBER
	I ATTENDED DECEDENT SINCE 1972	Robert O. ...	A 07202
	LAST SAW DECEDENT ALIVE Oct 17, 1980	28E. TYPE PHYSICIANS NAME Robert ... M.D. Box 868 Redding Calf	

INJURY INFORMATION	29. SPECIFY ACCIDENT, SUICIDE, ETC.	30. PLACE OF INJURY	31. INJURY AT WORK	33A. DATE OF INJURY	32B. HOUR
	33. LOCATION		34. DESCRIBE HOW INJURY OCCURRED		

CORONER'S USE ONLY	35A. I CERTIFY THAT DEATH OCCURRED AT THE HOUR, DATE AND PLACE STATED FROM THE CAUSES STATED	35B. CORONER—SIGNATURE AND DEGREE OR TITLE	35C. DATE SIGNED

	36. DISPOSITION	37. DATE	38. NAME AND ADDRESS OF CEMETERY OR CREMATORY	39. EMBALMER'S LICENSE NUMBER AND SIGNATURE
	Cremains Buried	10-27-80	Private Property - Shasta County	Not Embalmed
	40. NAME OF FUNERAL DIRECTOR	41. LOCAL REGISTRAR—SIGNATURE		42. DATE ACCEPTED BY LOCAL REGISTRAR
	Walter Simonis	Rebecca Ashmun, Deputy Register		JAN 9 1981
STATE REGISTRAR	A.	B.	C.	D.	E.	F.

VS-11 (10-78)

Robert Simonis' death certificate – 1980

Elizabeth Simonis' headstone at family gravesite

Robert Simonis with youngest daughter Hester, and grandchildren Buck, Sallie, and Robert – 1975.

PART THREE

Chapter 1

Calls to the Coroner

We figured that the time was passing, and we'd better call the coroner's office to let them know that Mr. Simonis had died. Everyone was so upset; we weren't ready to give him up, and we hadn't thought about what we would do with his body when he died. We were still waiting for some of the family to arrive at the house. We had no plans of our own except to do what the doctor had told us to do. There was some confusion among us because of the conflict between Dr. Jantzen's orders, and now calling in the coroner. Aunt Cody looked up the phone number. She made the call. The telephone rang and the call was answered by the answering service. Cody knew the procedure so she gave her name, phone number, and the reason for her call. The operator said she would put her right through to the deputy coroner who was a woman by the name of Maude Brody; the coroner was off duty for the night she said. Cody was asked to hold on the line and she would be connected as soon as possible.

As Cody was waiting, the phone clicked in and a sleepy voice said, "Maude Brody here."

Cody explained who she was and what the call was about. She said the reason for her call was that Dr. Ryalls had suggested she call the coroner to report Mr. Simonis' death. Cody tried to give her a shortened version of what had just occurred with Mr. Simonis' death, but she was interrupted.

"What is the address?"

Cody gave her the address and when she finished, the phone went dead.

Cody hung up the phone on her end and said with a quizzical expression, "She was either real sleepy or just a plain grouch!"

It seemed as though time was standing still while waiting for the coroner. There was a loud knock at the front door. My mother answered the door. There was a man and a woman standing there. The woman had very short hair and appeared to be dressed in men's clothing. She spoke with a rough manner of authority and identified herself only as the deputy coroner. She said she was covering for the coroner, Joseph Cann, who was off-duty. Glancing over to the side of them, Mother observed that she had brought several vehicles with her. There was a rescue unit consisting of a fire truck, ambulance, and a policeman. They were all driving their vehicles in front of the house. Ms. Brody never identified the man next to her.

She stated as she pushed her way though the door, "Where is the body?"

She acted as though she was mechanically on a mission.

Mother said, "Please follow me," and escorted her to the bedroom where Dad was lying.

The house was always clean, but Mother had a tendency to pile things around. There never seemed to be enough room even though it was a large four-bedroom house. We did have to rearrange some things so that Dad could be cared for easier. As Mother guided her down the crowded hallway, she apologized for the mess and for Dr. Ryalls.

She said, "He was supposed to come to the house when my husband passed. I'm sorry that he had put this onto you in the middle of the night."

Very nicely and nervously, Mother rambled on. Ms. Brody never replied. Several members of the family in the room with Dad moved aside for her as she entered. Maude Brody never looked at one person in the room; she just affixed her focus on Dad's body on the bed. She walked straight to him with her clipboard in hand. She pulled the sheet back exposing his clothed body. She felt his arm for a pulse, looked into his eyes, and then looked his body over from front to back without ever saying a word. She wrote something quickly on her clipboard. Then she picked up a pillow that was sitting next to the bed and covered my dad's face with it. You can imagine the family's reaction. I was horrified! Here we were all sadly watching as she examined our father and she puts a pillow on his face when she's done. We all gasped and lunged towards the bed.

I pulled the pillow off his face saying, "What are you doing?"

She never reacted. She was cold and impersonal. She acted like this was the way it was always done. If she had pulled the sheet up over his face, I believe it would have been more acceptable to us. However, I don't think we would have liked that either.

She turned around looking for my mother, and said, "I have some papers that need to be filled out."

Mother had gone out of the room while Maude Brody was examining Dad. Strength has a lot to do with love, but understandably, there were things about my father's demise that my mother couldn't or didn't want to have to deal with. When Mother saw her coming down the hall, she said that she would answer any questions that she had.

Mother answered all of her questions at the kitchen table. I was still in the bedroom discussing quietly with my family this woman's disconcerting attitude toward my father's death. My emotions were shattered; I thought what kind of a woman would treat people in this manner who had just lost their father after a grave illness?

I overheard my mother raising her voice in the kitchen, so I went to see if everything was all right. Aunt Cody told me that apparently Maude Brody said she was taking Bob's body for "inspection!" I heard Mother ask her to call Dr. Ryalls, and he would give her the entire medical history along with any information that she needed on Dad. She needed. to clear up any ideas she might be having because she said very distinctly, "You are not taking my husband's body anywhere."

Ms. Brody refused to call the doctor and threatened my mother with arrest if she didn't release "The Body." Mother didn't back down. Her demeanor changed, and she calmly told her to call her superior, Coroner Mr. Cann. Ms. Brody snapped back that she didn't have to do that. She stated that she had complete authority in this case and any other case that came up tonight.

She persisted and said again, "If you don't release the body to me, I don't think you will like the consequences. I will arrest you and maybe everyone else in this house will be arrested, too."

Mother called her bluff and said that she would have to arrest them then, because she wasn't handing her husband over to anyone at this time! It was a stand-off for a moment. Finally, Ms. Brody went to the door and called a police officer into our home. She instructed him to watch over "the body," as she referred to Dad. She then went to the phone and called the coroner. After talking for several minutes to Mr. Cann, she hung up the phone.

She said to Mother, "Okay, now I've talked to Mr. Cann as you wanted me to, and he says I need to take "the body" with me."

I held my breath. We all did. Was she going to arrest Mother? We knew Mother wasn't going to give in to her. We stood behind our mother on pins and needles. When Mother refused, she said she was leaving and would leave a policeman in the house to watch over "the body" until she returned.

She went to the front door and ordered the policeman from outside to come in and stay inside to watch the body. Then she left. The policeman stood in the kitchen with this whole houseful of distressed people. He didn't say anything. He just looked rather displaced in the middle of all this. There was always a pot of coffee brewing, so I asked him if he wanted a cup, but he declined it. He never left the kitchen area, but he could see straight down the hall into the bedroom. In the bedroom, the work had begun to prepare Dad's body. The boys lovingly worked on adjusting his body. Si shaved and cleaned him; they put his dentures in his mouth and focused a lot of attention on keeping his eyes closed. Soon after death, the body starts a process called rigor mortis, which is caused by a chemical change in the muscles. It causes the limbs of the corpse to become stiff and difficult to move or manipulate. Rigor usually occurs within three or four hours after clinical death, with full rigor being in effect in about twelve hours. The body eventually subsides and relaxes at about thirty-six hours after death. So they had to start working on Dad to make sure he was presentable for viewing. It was of vital importance to begin immediately, since Dad had already been dead two or three hours by now.

Si had gone earlier in the week to see his old scout master, Ruben Kencade, who just happened to work for a mortuary. Si hadn't told us this until after Dad had died. Ruben had instructed Si in just what to do with Dad's body to preserve it. He said to clean and adjust the body after Dad died; to make sure his face looked presentable if we were going to view him with an open casket service. He told Si to pack dry ice in towels around the torso of his body under his clothes. If the dry ice touched his skin it would burn the skin, he said. Si's plan was to build Dad's coffin and keep his body in it for three days at home. I thought to bring it to the crematorium for cremation after we had his funeral. He said Ruben was very supportive with what he had enquired about doing and was helpful as well. Before Si left, Rubin reminded him that the death certificate was of the utmost importance.

By law, he said, "Your father's body legally belongs to your mother, but to be able to keep it, she must have a death certificate signed by the doctor in attendance or an official of the law, which is the law."

The boys now had Dad's body cleaned, dressed, and laid out in a clean bed awaiting the coroner's decision. We didn't know what we were going to do, but we didn't want to let our dad go yet. It was after three in the morning, and the rest of the family had arrived at the house by now. It was a very depressing scene. Our dad had just died after a long battle with cancer. There was a policeman in the house standing guard over him, with more policemen outside. A deputy coroner had threatened the arrest of our whole family.

When the doctor passed his responsibility to the coroner's office, instead of doing his job, it set off the unfortunate chain of events that were progressing against us by the minute. My family was being treated like criminals that had done something sinister to our father.

While waiting, I remember saying to my sister, Mary, "Do they think we killed our dad?"

She said, "Don't say that. Aren't we having enough trouble without them hearing that word out of one of us?"

This was unbelievable. Here was my whole family—a mother, thirteen kids, many with families of their own, a grandmother, and an aunt—overwhelmed with grief over the death of this man. The events of the evening had escalated in such a short period of time into making us feel as though we had done something wrong by caring for him.

Meanwhile, as we all tried to comfort each other while waiting, Aunt Cody was trying to distract and comfort Mother in the living room with stories of Bob's adventures. She wanted to keep her from worrying about what the next action might be from that cold-hearted Maude Brody. She had just turned Mother's world upside down and frightened most of the family.

Suddenly, as they were talking, the living room door flew open without a knock. Ms. Brody walked right into the house. First, she directed her attention to the policeman and ordered his relief of his duty to the body. She then turned and walked back to the open door.

She said, "I have talked with the coroner again, and he will be in contact with you later this morning."

She walked out the door without closing it behind her and went straight to her car. I ran and closed the door. Then I hurried to the laundry room window, which obstructed the view of the inside of the house from the outside, and I watched as all of the police, firemen, the ambulance, and Ms. Brody drove away. What a relief that was to feel safe again, at least for awhile.

All of us stayed at the house for the rest of the night. It was a big house with a lot of room. There were beds in the carport where we sometimes slept when it was hot. I tried to get some sleep, but it seemed impossible. All the events of the night were playing over and over in my mind. We had many things to deal with in the next couple of hours, and a lot of decisions had to be made.

The family gathered about seven in the morning to decide what they had to do first. Of course, being the oldest, Si seemed to be the director of us all. Building the casket and getting the death certificate were first on the list of things to do. The brothers consulted each other as to how they would build Dad's coffin and what materials they would need. He had requested to just be put in a pine box and buried on the property, but I knew the boys were planning to do more than that.

It was nine o'clock Friday morning now. Aunt Cody called Dr. Ryalls' office to find out if one of my sisters could come to his office to pick up the death certificate. The secretary told Cody that the coroner's office usually had the papers sent over early, so they could be on the doctor's desk to sign when he came in. She said they were not there yet, and the doctor wasn't there. She said she would have the doctor call us as soon as he came in. Dr. Ryalls called back about 9:30, and said he had called the coroner's office. Apparently there was some hang-up about delivering the papers. The doctor suggested to her, that a member of the family could go to the coroner's office, pick up the papers, bring them to his office, and he would sign them. Cody said that was a good idea. She would send one of the older girls. Again all this seemed rather peculiar to Cody, but instead of waiting, she followed the doctor's orders. She sent my two sisters, Mary and

Phoebe, to go pick up the death certificate at the coroner's office and take it to Dr. Ryalls' office, so we hopefully wouldn't have anymore problems with the law.

The girls got to the coroner's office about 10:00 a.m. The secretary took their names, seated them, and said she would inform Mr. Cann that they were there. They waited nervously and relived the night before, but they didn't anticipate any trouble.

The girls, being deep in thought, didn't notice when a man entered the room and said in a loud nasty voice, "So, you're the people who woke me up in the middle of the night? Did you know I could have had you all arrested last night? I still might do that. In fact, I could have you two taken into custody right now if I wanted to."

This unexpected outburst startled both of them. Phoebe said it was like getting hit in the solar plexus. She couldn't understand the cruelness of his attack on them. Feeling sick to her stomach, she tried to regain her composure. Fighting back tears and anger, she explained to him that they were only following the doctor's orders in calling his office. She tried to tell him about the kind of man Robert Simonis was, including his lifestyle and his philosophy on life and death. Cann kept interrupting every word she tried to say. She continued talking through his attempts to interrupt her, and she told him that we were a responsible family. She was trying to give him a brief history of our dad's illness and care that he had been receiving. She wanted him to try to understand that we were upholding our father's dying wishes. She told the coroner that he could check the medical records with one quick phone call to resolve this unnecessary situation. Noticing he was getting more upset with her, she decided she would ask him for the death certificate as the doctor had requested. They needed to take it to Dr. Ryalls to have it signed.

Mr. Cann yelled at them, "There will be no death certificate until you people hand over Mr. Simonis' body for inspection."

He frightened them both so bad with that outburst that they both got up and left his office without saying another word and without the death certificate. They hurried to their car, and hoped he wasn't going to stop them and arrest them.

As they drove home, they discussed the meaning of the word "inspection." Did "inspection" mean they wanted to autopsy his body to determine the cause of death? We all knew the cause of death, and if they would listen, they would know the cause of death. This became more of a power play for their positions. My father's death did not qualify in any part of the coroner's department. The definition of a coroner is, "A public officer who investigates death by unnatural or unknown suspicious causes." My father's death was expected and medically cared for. The need for an "inspection," as the coroner called it, did not apply here.

Back at the house, everyone seemed a little jumpy. After such a threat as we had earlier, none of us would be at ease until we had the death certificate in our possession. There was heaviness in the air. I had a feeling as though I was waiting for some unknown catastrophe to happen. When Mary and Phoebe got back from the coroner's office without the certificate, I knew it had something to do with my uneasy feelings. I hoped that the doctor would have been able to get the death certificate for us; Cody would keep abreast of that. The household was busy getting ready for the news that our dad had passed in the night. The boys were at a friend's cabinetry shop building the coffin all day, while the rest of us cleaned the house and prepared food. Neighbors and friends began to call and bring food over. Some flowers arrived in the afternoon, and one of Dad's brothers came by. The news was out that Mr. Simonis had died, and the condolences were pouring in.

This day and into the evening was one of the most stressful days of my life. I was so mentally exhausted, and not only did I have this death and a funeral to deal with, but I also had the living—my children and my mother to worry about. I was very worried about my mother. She was strong, but she kept her feelings concealed inside. I didn't think that was good for her health. All of this would have been overwhelming for her if it hadn't been for the unity of this family.

To transfer Dad from the bed into the casket would be a very emotional task for all of us. I decided that I would stay the night at the house with Mother because it was late; my children were already asleep. In the morning, I could get more done from here. I fixed a bed in the living room with my baby and tried to sleep; people were sleeping everywhere in the house and outside in the carport. I was glad for the beds in the carport, because all the extra beds were filled. Everything seemed okay to go to sleep. Under Mother's supervision, the casket had been built and lined with Dad's white U.S. Navy blankets. The boys had closed the lid of the casket in the bedroom for the night. It really looked nice. It wasn't fancy; just a plain wooden coffin with brass handles that had been made by his sons with a lot of love. It was perfect for who Dad was.

Chapter 2
The Siege

I was awakened by my baby, Georgianna, who was starting to fuss and nudging me to nurse her. It was very uncomfortable on the floor of the living room. I didn't want the baby to wake anyone else, so I sat in my mother's rocking chair to nurse her. I looked at the clock on the fireplace, and it said 7:45. I was so tired from a night of unrest, and the whole household was still asleep as I nursed her. I kept closing my eyes and dozing off. I thought I heard a car drive up so I stretched up as far as I could to see out the window. From where I was sitting, I could only see half of the yard and the street outside. My mother never had curtains on her windows; I was moving myself in the chair carefully so that Georgianna didn't drop her nipple. That's when I noticed one, two, and then three white roofs of cars pulling into the front of the house. My parents lived on a residential street that dead-ended, so I thought this was pretty strange to see on a Saturday morning at this time. I got up from the chair while holding the baby in my arms, and I was shocked by a barrage of white sheriff's cars stopping in front of the house. For a second it didn't registered with me that it was the police and they were coming to this house. My first consideration was for my family; do not wake them. In literally seconds, a fire truck and city police cars arrived, along with a swat team who began pouring out of a van. They were dressed in uniforms, all carrying weapons, filing toward and around the house. A man dressed in casual clothes carrying some sort of iron bar led the party with one large police officer at his side. They stormed up the front walkway to the front door of the house. I was frozen in shear horror. It was like watching a slow motion movie that had you immobilized. My mother was asleep on a mattress across from me in front of the living room door, along with many other people in the living room.

I yelled to Mother under my breath in a sort of whisper, "Wake up, Mother. There are police everywhere!"

Just at that moment, there was a pounding at the door in front of me, and a heavy voice said, "This is the Shasta County Coroner. Open the door. I have come for Mr. Simonis' body."

I jumped backward and nearly fell over; it startled me so bad that my baby began to cry. Mother, in her dazed sleep, was trying to get to her feet.

"Don't open the door, Georgia," she mumbled groggily.

I yelled back through the door, "No, I can't open it; you will have to wait for my mother to come to the door," thinking that might give Mother a minute to compose herself.

"Open the door! If you don't, you had better get out of the way, because I am coming through it. I will break it down and someone is going to get hurt!" he yelled back.

I was standing right in front of the door.

Looking down at my baby, and shaking, I yelled, "You'd better not. I have a baby in my arms."

I jumped backwards, almost frantic now, and felt the danger for my baby and myself.

I said to Mother, "They've surrounded the house. This household is completely under siege. There are cops everywhere. They were going around the back of the house before he came to the door."

Never to this day have I been so frightened for my life, the lives of my children, my mother, my grandmother, and my family. Mother was now stumbling to her feet. Propelled by the excitement in his voice, she opened the window next to the door where Mr. Cann was standing with a bar in his hand, and she said very calmly, "Mr. Cann, do you have a search warrant?"

"I don't need one! You open the door. I want that body," he said.

At times like these, I wonder why I worry about my mother's strength. Thankfully, Mother was very familiar with the law, and had demanded a search warrant from him.

She said, "If I am to open my door, I demand to see your search warrant first, sir. Otherwise, PLEASE step off my property."

This stopped him dead in his tracks. He stood there speechless, but we could see him thinking. This was going to slow his pursuit down a little. He turned to talk to the police officer that was behind him, and then they walked to the edge of the street. Four officers joined them, and with the coroner, they talked amongst themselves. Two officers went to their patrol cars and got on the radio. The others followed the coroner back into the yard. They now stood about ten feet from our front door. My mother said later that she figured with her demand for a legal search warrant, that his attempt to coerce her unlawfully had failed. He didn't have a search warrant with him; at least not one signed by a judge. However, he was now attempting to get one.

While my mother watched their every move, she said, "We need help, Georgia. Call Dr. Jantzen's home, and see if he has returned. If he doesn't answer, call the media and tell them to send out a reporter to this house."

Everyone was now waking up in the house. It was mayhem; my aunt was trying to take care of them all. My sister, Mary, and me were on the telephone trying desperately to get someone to help us. I thought that if there were witnesses, like the press, who saw what was happening to us, that perhaps the coroner would be more careful and not blast through the front door endangering the whole family. Either she, or I, would take turns calling on the phone. I called the local TV media and radio stations. I asked them to send out reporters. I called Dr. Jantzen's home [he wasn't scheduled to return to town until the next day, but we were grabbing at straws for a miracle that he might answer]. Mary reached a TV station out of Chico, a nearby town, and they said they would send a reporter out. She also called Si and Phoebe, who hadn't stayed the night at our parent's house. Between each call, we would dial Dr. Jantzen's phone. We prayed he would answer. [At the time, there weren't answering machines as there are now.]

I was telephoning at the front window when I saw Si drive up. There wasn't a parking place due to the nine police cars in front of the house. He parked across the street several houses away. A policeman immediately approached him as he came close to the house and asked his name. Si identified himself and said he was going into the house. Two other policemen hurried over, and they grabbed and handcuffed Si. They put him in the back seat of a police car without giving him a chance to speak or object. From my viewpoint, Si didn't offer any resistance to the policemen, yet I couldn't hear what they were saying to each other. As we were watching this scene, my mother ran to the back door, opened it, and ran through the police line that circled the carport. She was crying and yelling at the police, completely hysterical, "release my son." Not only was her whole family under a dangerous volatile police siege, now these policemen had handcuffed and arrested her oldest son in front of her eyes. For what?

She was yelling, "Let him go, let him go!"

As she reached the end of her driveway, one of the policemen stepped in front of her to stop her from reaching the police car. Just then, my sister, Margaret, caught up to her and brought her back into the house. Margaret, Sookie, Nellie, and Hester had been the ones sleeping in the carport when the siege started. They awoke to uniformed cops with guns above their heads. They had been too afraid to move. My brother-in-law brought them into the house after it all started. This was a volatile situation for all of us. Mother was so upset that she went back to the window and yelled at Cann that they better not hurt her son. The girls tried to calm her down; they were afraid the stress could cause her to have a heart attack or something worse.

Each room throughout the house had one of us guarding the windows. Aunt Cody had taken the small children to the back of the house and put them in one of the bedrooms for their protection. I didn't know if the police were going to break down the doors and the windows. I tried not to scare the children too much. We made light of the police at both the windows outside of the room. From the phone in the hallway, I called my ex-husband who lived close by. I told him to come immediately and pick up our two boys, as I feared for their lives. I didn't know if the police would let them leave, but I was going to try. He came very quickly, and my sister, Liz, told me he had arrived when she saw him park down the road by the creek. He came walking up through the neighbor's yard. I took the boys to the back door, and told the policeman that I was sending my boys with their father for their safety. The policemen let them pass without a word.

I kissed them both and said, "Go with your Dad and have some fun. Mom will see you tomorrow."

I felt a sense of relief knowing they would be safe now, but my heart hurt. I didn't know if I would ever see them again. I came back inside the house, and I went to the back room to check on the other kids whom I had left with Auntie Hester. They were hiding in the bottom of a large walk-in closet with the door open. Hester was playing with them and they seemed to think it was a great game.

I said, "Just stay in here with Auntie Hester, and I'll be back."

From there, I went to the next bedroom to check on Dad in his casket. His casket was still sitting on the bed where the boys had left it. Nellie, Henry and Sookie were on guard there. I could see through the windows that the police had surrounded the house and weren't more than six feet apart from one another. Sookie and Henry whispered to me that the police had removed the screens from both of the windows in the room. I told them if anyone came near the windows to come and get us immediately. Maybe the police were just trying to see if they could see a dead body, or maybe they had been given orders to take the screens off; I don't know. Cautiously, I went to both windows and made sure they were locked. The policemen outside just stood there and looked at me like robots. This was one time I wished my mother had put curtains on the windows; none of the windows in my parent's home ever had curtains on them. My mother would say that the kids sometimes used the windows more than the doors, and the curtains just got in our way. I know my sisters and I had a lot of visitors at our bedroom windows and the boy's room was like a freeway at times. I instructed my brother and sisters to stand guard at the bedroom door, but not inside the room, in case the police tried to come through the windows. I knew that this all sounded crazy but nothing seemed beyond belief now. Anything was possible. Before this happened, I had never been so frightened or fearful for my life as on that October morning. Just to write this story, and to relive that horrendous experience, brings back all of those feelings of fear just like it happened that morning.

We had kept Nanny's bedroom door closed. I opened it and peeked in; she was sound asleep. She probably hadn't gone to bed until it was morning. Because she was eighty years old, it was best to keep her unaware of what was happening in the rest of the house if possible. If she had awakened and seen the police at her window, only God knows what would have happened to her.

The hell I was living in continued in the front of the house as I returned. I could see through the front window that there was more commotion again at the street. Phoebe had just arrived and was coming into the yard when a large policeman stood in front of her and ordered her to stop. She identified herself and said that her ten-year-old daughter, Sarah, was inside the house, and she needed to go in to be with her. The policeman told her she could not enter the perimeter of the property, and if she didn't get back, he would arrest her. As mad and upset as Phoebe was, she didn't want to be arrested. She just stood in the street yelling to anyone who would listen.

When a car passed, the house she yelled, "Help us. Look what the coroner and police are unlawfully doing to my family."

The neighbors across the street were peeking out their windows but didn't come out. I later found out that the neighbor directly across the street from the house took notes of all the events that happened that morning. She recorded everything from the time the siege started, and presented her notes as evidence to the grand jury's inquest that was conducted later.

This policeman treated Phoebe's approach to the house entirely different from how his colleague treated Si's approach to the house. Someone from inside the house yelled out to Phoebe to go back to her car; they said the police have already arrested Si. She didn't know that just minutes before Si had been arrested, and that he was sitting in a police car helplessly watching this "siege" on the family a few feet away from her.

The next vehicle coming up the street had a local TV station's logo on the door. It felt to me as though the calvary had arrived, and it gave me a sensation of hope. Poni went to the back door to welcome the newsperson as I continued her job of calling on the telephone. Mother kept an eye on the coroner who was pacing back and forth near his car in the front yard. Getting out of the car was a female reporter who worked for the local television station. Three of my sisters, Nellie, Margaret, and Hester, had danced with this woman, so they knew her and she knew our family.

Poni said to her, "Thank you for coming. Please come in. My mother would like you to see firsthand what is happening here."

The woman stopped and put her hand up to Poni, saying, "Why don't you people do what's right and turn that body over to the coroner?"

Poni looked at her in shock. She was a news reporter who should have been there to report a newsworthy event, regardless of her personal opinion. She was supposed to be an unbiased part of the news. On the contrary; she refused the invitation to come in the house. She said she would be out front. She went and stood by a sheriff deputy. She never took any notes or interviewed anyone during the siege. I later found out that this woman was married to a sheriff deputy. That's probably why she took the stance against us that she did. This story turned into worldwide news, and this reporter had the chance to have the exclusive, which she missed out on.

After an hour-and-a-half of total terror, the telephone rang. It startled Mary as she was just reaching for the phone to make another call.

She answered the phone, and on the other end of the line she heard, "Hello, this is Dr. Jantzen."

It was our family doctor calling. What a miracle!

Mary was temporarily speechless but recovered quickly saying, "Dr. Jantzen, can you hold the line? We have an emergency here. I'll get my mother."

Mary yelled through the house, "Mother, Dr. Jantzen is on the phone."

Mother came from the kitchen and took the phone, which Mary had outstretched as far as it would go. Very quickly, she explained to the doctor the predicament the family was in with the coroner's "siege." The doctor listened intensely and calmly.

Without hesitation, he said, "Put the coroner on the phone, please!"

Still not taking the chance of opening the front door and inviting this man in, Mother opened the window, tore off the screen, and said to the coroner, who was standing a few feet away, "Mr. Cann, this phone call is for you. It's Dr. Jantzen."

Mary and I were standing over Mother's shoulder. Mr. Cann looked puzzled at the telephone.

Then he took it from her and spoke into it, "Joseph Cann here."

You could have heard a pin drop; there was complete silence inside and out. Every eye was on the coroner. He listened for only a few moments, and then he spoke very quietly.

I heard him say, "Yes, yes, all right."

He handed the phone back to my mother who had been almost hanging out the window trying to hear Mr. Cann's side of the conversation. She put the phone up to her ear, and the doctor reassured her that everything would be all right now. He said he told the coroner he would sign the death certificate as soon as the coroner brought the papers out to him. He reassured her again that everything would be all right. He said that he was outside cutting wood, which made him think of Bob. He called as soon as he was finished. He apologized for the trouble, and said if she needed anything else to just call him.

She had to laugh at that, and said, "You don't know how many times the girls have called you this morning. Thank you so much, doctor."

She hung up the phone. Looking out the window, she still wondered what the coroner would do next, since he was just standing and watching her. The doctor's phone call gave her legal right to her husband's body. This gave her some peace of mind, except that her yard was still full of police, and her son was still sitting across the street in a police car.

The coroner stood expressionless in the yard for a few minutes. He knew he was defeated by the doctor's call. His illegal and costly siege to get Mr. Simonis' body had backfired on him. We all stood at the windows watching; he walked to the edge of the street where the police officers and the newswoman were waiting. They stood there conversing as if they were deciding where to go for coffee. Inside the house, we were still being held hostage by the coroner. We waited.

Was this over yet? Mother told us to be very quiet and to stay alert. Another twenty minutes went by as the coroner and the large officer stood in the street next to their cars. I was watching every move that was made out there through the now screenless front window. I could see the officer talking on his police radio, and then the coroner got into his car and just drove away.

The policeman appeared to talk some more on the radio, and then he put out an order to all officers to "abort the mission." The attack was over. The police passed the word and started dispersing immediately from the yard and street. They loaded into their many cars and vans and drove away. The firemen who had been sitting in the fire truck the whole time, left in their big red truck. The reporter left in her newsworthy vehicle, and the many onlookers who had gathered and lined the street began leaving, too. Phoebe came running into the yard and into the house. The police car that had Si in the back seat left with him in it. We hoped they would release him before they left, but they needed something to show for such a large-scale abuse of power paid for by the people. There was a semi-feeling of relief among us, as we looked back and forth to each other. However, there wasn't time yet to relax. We now had the task of getting Si out of jail.

We wondered what Si would be charged with. He never did anything but try to walk up to the house. Mother called the jail a few minutes later and asked if he was being arrested. If so, she asked how much his bail would be. They said he was being charged with obstructing justice, and there would be a bail of $2,500.00 on him. She told them that her son was in perfect condition when the police put him in the police car. She said she expected him to be released in the same condition. Hanging up the phone, she sent his wife, Melinda, into the police station to bail him out.

I stayed close to the house hoping there wouldn't be another attack on us. I was still in disbelief of what had just occurred here this morning. It now felt as if it were a dream; a nightmare of a dream, but a dream nonetheless. I couldn't help but to ask myself what happened here today; what did we do wrong? Why was taking care of our dead father such a crime? All of these questions needed answering but now wasn't the time. It was a miracle that none of us were hurt or killed, and I thanked God again and again for that. Our grandmother had slept through the whole "siege," and we still had Dad in the bedroom in his casket. As I thought about all of this, it was sad what they had done to my family. I felt weak. But my feelings had to wait, too. I didn't have the luxury of a collapse or breakdown right now. I didn't even have time to mourn the loss of my father; it had been taken away from me that morning.

Chapter 3
The Preparation

Si was bailed and released from the jail after being fingerprinted and booked. He and Melinda came straight back to my parent's home. When he came through the living room door, Mother embraced him with a hold only a mother herself would understand. She watched helplessly an hour before as the police handcuffed him, put him in their car, and drove away with him. Tears came pouring out of her eyes onto his shoulder now, and she wept with uncontrollable sobs. Si stood with his strong arms around her, while she just let all of the fear, the sadness, and the loneliness of the last months come roaring out of her. Her emotional well-being had reached its limit; this was the last draw attacking her home and children. Overcome by these emotions, she continued to sob in Si's arms. With this siege of injustices, and secure in her oldest son's arms, she somehow felt the strength to go through all of this and whatever more there was to come. She said she received a message as she was being held in his arms; she knew that things would only get better from this time forward. Call it psychic, but somehow she just knew everything would be all right from then on.

The day progressed without anymore unwelcome visitors. I was still looking over my shoulder; we all were. Many friends called and stopped by the house after hearing the news of the "siege" on the family. It was all over the TV news broadcast and radio. This was a small town that I had grown up in, and any family that had thirteen kids was pretty well-known by most people. The schools still to this day have Simonis children enrolled in them.

Keeping a watchful eye of who was coming and going, I noticed a car with a young man slowly driving past the house. He parked across the street two houses down. He got out of his car. He was dressed in Levis and a striped shirt; closing the door behind him, he opened the back car door and took out a plant. With the plant in his hand, he came slowly down the street toward the house. Something about his demeanor didn't look like your average delivery person. While walking up the sidewalk to the front door, he looked nervous, and he was fidgeting with the plant. He rang the doorbell and I answered it.

He said, "Hello, my name is John Parr. I'm one of the police officers that had been involved in "the raid" on your family's home earlier this morning."

I just stared at him.

"I'm here because I would like the family to accept this plant."

He handed me the plant.

"It's a small token of my personal apologies for my part in the raid."

I probably looked very surprised and a little suspicious. I took the plant with some apprehension, and I thanked him.

He explained, "I was just doing my job. When my squadron was briefed for the assignment this morning, we were only told that we were going to a location where a man had died the day before, and the family would not give up his dead body. We were here to assist the coroner in retrieving that body if needed. I personally didn't know what to expect from this assignment. I had an image in my mind of a dead man laying somewhere in a house or something worse. With little or no information, your mind starts to wander and adds its own pictures," he said.

I said, "Well, thank you again."

However, he still continued by saying, "I was in the back of the house. I took the screen off the window and was very surprised when I saw a normal bedroom."

He stopped.

"Well, not normal with a coffin on the bed, but you know what I mean. Anyhow, the hand-tailored coffin and the flowers; it wasn't what I was expecting to find. I questioned the orders in my mind at the time as to why we were here at this family's heartbreaking time," he said.

He continued, "I think I saw you and I presume some of the other family members frantically running back and forth checking on the casket. I felt ashamed then, and I feel ashamed now for my part in the raid. It bothered me so much. I just wanted you to know it."

I told him that I appreciated his honesty and courage to be able to come here and tell us that. Mr. Parr backed away with a slight bow of his head and humbly left the yard. Several of my sisters had gathered around the door and were listening to this man. We watched as he got into his car and left. It took a lot of courage, I thought, to come here. I was moved and thankful that someone in all this madness gave my family a little credit for our efforts at being responsible for our loved one.

Things in the house started to settle down towards evening. Now it was time to get back to the care of Dad's body. He had gone through many transformations in his last days of life. I saw the results of when his regular thinking changed; spiritually, something different happened within him; not only his loving words but also in his expressions and actions. He was truly sincere and sorry for his behavior of not being more involved in all of our upbringing. He was mostly sorry for not telling us children that he loved us more. My dad was never a mean man; please don't get me wrong when I say that. He just came to realize there is more to raising a family than providing income.

The boys went to their friend at the mortuary and borrowed a casket stand for us to use at the funeral service. We decided it would give us more room in the bedroom to take the bed out and put Dad's casket on the stand. Then when people came by, like they had been doing all day, there would be more room and it would look more professional, like we knew what we were doing. The boys picked the casket up with Dad inside to move it from the bed to the floor, and then from the floor to the stand after they had removed the bed from the room. As I was arranging the flowers on top of the casket, I noticed that there was a large vein raised in the middle of Dad's forehead. It was vividly protruding out. It wasn't noticeable before we moved him. It lumped up and I thought it looked like he was angry. I commented on it, making a joke of it amongst us.

I said, "I guess Dad must be mad at us for moving him out of his bed."

We all agreed that this had changed his expression.

Around six o'clock that evening, some very good friends of my dad's, Jim and Melba, came to the house to visit and pay their respects. They brought food, a beautiful wreath of flowers, and some welcomed encouraging words for us. We escorted them to the bedroom where we had Dad. I set up the flowers with the many others in the room. Melba remarked that the coffin was perfectly beautiful, and it fit Bob's personality perfect. My dad had always enjoyed Jim's company. He had logged and sold Christmas trees with Jim for many years. All of my brothers, who had worked with and for Jim, joined in and gathered around the casket. Soon we were all in and out of the room telling our favorites stories about Dad. Jim shared many stories of their adventures that literally had us in stitches laughing. Sometimes we cried with joy. It was a very good evening for all of us. It's amazing what joy and laughter can do for your spirit when you least expect it. I know that it raised my spirit. It had been so long since I was able to laugh in Dad's presence. While they were still sitting around the casket, I left the room to get something to eat. I could hear Jim and my brothers telling jokes and laughing. I went back into the room when I was finished eating. I peered into the casket at Dad, only to be surprised that the lumped-up vein that had been protruding from Dad's forehead had softened and disappeared. A peaceful serenity had come over his face. I couldn't hold back my reaction for them to finish talking.

I just jumped in, and I said, "Oh my gosh! Look, you guys. The lump on Dad's forehead is gone! He isn't mad at us anymore."

We all could see the change in his expression and appearance. It was a little eerie, but it made me feel good. When Dad passed away, he looked ninety years old. Now he looked his age or younger. I know that Dad's spirit was celebrating with all of us there in that room. It was undeniable to each of us the love that penetrated through all of our hearts at that moment. My belief is that the spirit/soul stays close to the body for a period of time after death. The spirit/soul has to have time to get used to the idea that it is not connected with the body anymore, and each day gives it a degree more of separation from the body. My family and I were witnessing this transformation in his face that brought such peace to us. We may not have witnessed this, and we would have missed this unbelievable experience if he were not there with us caring for him.

I was feeling so good about the evening and the fact that nothing had happened the rest of the day that I decided I would go home to sleep instead of staying at the house that night. My husband and family needed me, too. Mother now had a signed death certificate in her possession, even though it was not recorded with the county yet, because of the day being Saturday, but she had it. I felt positive everything would be all right. I could go home and sleep tonight; sleep had evaded me since Dad's death. I still had some worries regarding the "hows" of all that the family had left to do. How would we pull the rest of this off? How were we going to get Dad in the casket out of the house and up the hill to the mountains? How were we going to stay away from the law if they decided to attack again? There were still many unanswered questions, and things had to be done. However, it didn't seem to matter right now. I was mentally and physically fatigued, and it was time to sleep. My dad had given me a gift this evening that could not be bought. I had the peace of mind that he was all right. He was there in spirit with his family, and he had received the love we were sending out to him. My heart felt the love and security that I knew he had received. So yes, I did sleep. I had my first completely restful night of sleep in weeks.

I woke up to the smell of bacon cooking. I could hear my husband, Kim, trying to keep our boys quiet so they would not wake me. Georgianna was lying next to me sound asleep. Her regular routine had been upset, and she was as exhausted as I was. I looked out the window to see the sun shining, when all of a sudden a memory came to me. Dad had come to me in a dream in the night. I wondered if it was real, or if I had dreamed it. He sat by my bed and stroked my hair.

He talked to me telepathically, and said, "All will be well."

I picked up the telephone and called my parent's home. Aunt Cody answered the phone and said that all was well there. Wow, I got that eerie feeling again.

"No problems through the night," she said. That was good news. It was also validation for me that Dad had come to me in my dream and said almost those same words. I smiled to myself. I had anticipated it would be another stressful day, but I knew now I could do it and all would be well. I got out of bed, and I got dressed. I went out and ate the breakfast Kim had cooked for me. Then I started to get the kids ready to go to my parent's house. He told me to leave the boys with him, and they'd do something fun like go fishing. What a relief that was not to have to worry about them right now. So I took the baby and went to my mother's house.

CHAPTER 4
CATCH 22

Driving to my mother's house, I noticed what a quiet Sunday morning it was. Hardly anyone was on the roads. It gave me time to think over some of the day's events. I was deep in thought when baby Georgianna made a little noise. I had almost forgotten that she was in the car with me asleep. I was looking forward to taking care of my family again. I arrived at the house, and most of the family was already there. Of course, my first thought was about Dad. Was he still safe in the bedroom? The next line of business was for us girls and Mother to discuss what we would do for the funeral service. The property was thirty miles away in the mountains. Would people be willing to drive up there for the funeral? We discussed all different options. One was that maybe it would be easier all around to have the service in town at the house instead. I thought that this might be much safer and easier on all of us. Then after the service, we could have the mortuary come to the house and pick up Dad's body. We could have him cremated the next day.

When I presented this idea to my brothers, their answer came back emphaticically, "No! We're going to follow Dad's wishes. We'll have him cremated, and then we'll bury him at the property. We'll have his service there, too. You girls worry about all the things that have to be done to put on the funeral, and we'll worry about how we'll get Dad there."

But what if the authorities try to stop us?" I asked.

"Don't worry about that, and don't say that in front of Mother," one of the boys said. "She doesn't need to be worrying anymore than she has to."

"Okay," I said, remembering my dream. "All will be well."

This was the first time I had heard anyone say anything about cremation. The plan, if we had a plan at all, I thought was to have Dad cremated and his ashes buried at the property. Now the original plans had changed and had taken on a life of their own. After all the horrific, illegal injustices the coroner had perpetrated on us, my brothers didn't trust Dad's body out of their sight. They had a plan in progress that they hadn't told me, or any of us, about until now. They were going to try to fool the authorities if they in fact might still be after Dad's body, into not knowing where his body was. The family had received several reports since the siege, from different sources, that undercover police cars were parked around our neighborhood and across the boulevard watching my parent's home. Because of the news coverage this case had gotten, the family was receiving calls from people volunteering their help and services. Si had one call from a family friend of my father's who owned and drove an ambulance. He volunteered his vehicle to transport Dad's body to the property, if we needed it. He enlightened us to the legal fact that anyone transporting a dead body must have a special license to do so. With his offer to help us, it would be easy enough and legal for him to drive the body in his ambulance. At the same time, we also found out through some unknown caller who said they worked for the county, that to be able to bury someone in a private unestablished cemetery, you must have five already dead bodies to establish a private cemetery. This was a complete catch-22. So it was legal to establish a private cemetery on your property, but to bury a person in it, you would have to have five dead people all at once, according to the way the law was set up. How would anyone establish a private cemetery anywhere? Where would the five dead people come from? All that I could figure was that this was enacted into law to keep people from burying people in their yards. I can understand that our society can't have people just burying someone anywhere, but at the same time, the law needs to take into account that if one goes through the right legal channels, then one death should be sufficient to be able to establish a private family cemetery on a prescribed amount of land (acres), not five deaths. So legally, to make a private family cemetery on your land, there should be a better way than burying five dead bodies all at once.

CHAPTER 5
A MOUNTAIN FUNERAL

The boys backed all the vehicles into the carport, the front yard, and the side yard of the house. There were two ambulances, three station wagons, and a van. The way the house was set up, the yard had a deep carport and low shade trees that obstructed the view to the back door of the house from the street. From a distance, if there was an onlooker, we probably looked like ants milling back and forth that morning. We were all busy loading the cars with food, flowers, music, pictures, dishes, some family members, tables and chairs, and more. We had everything we needed for the memorial service that would be transported to the mountains. Loading the vehicles had taken us most of the early part of the day. We had been instructed by the boys to use the tables as shields while we were loading, so that they could load the casket into one of the ambulances. We hoped that if anyone undercover was watching us, they wouldn't be able to tell which vehicle the casket or anything else went into. We checked and double-checked everything we thought we would need for the service, and then we huddled together for last minute instructions before anyone would drive away. It was decided that we were all to leave the house at the same time, and we'd take different routes to get to the property. Our plan was to confuse whoever was watching the house. We'd have more vehicles going in different directions than they did, if anyone was to follow. I left the yard in my station wagon, behind the ambulance that carried Dad's casket. Liz left behind the other ambulance. All the rest of the vehicles followed out of the driveway going different directions as they turned onto the main roadway. I didn't notice any suspicious vehicles as we entered the main road, but then I didn't know what kind of a vehicle I was watching for. I was so nervous; I just kept in mind what Dad had said in my dream. About a mile up the highway, a sheriff's car pulled in between the ambulance and my car. I was preparing myself for him to pull the ambulance over, but he just stayed behind it. We continued up the highway, and then turned onto the Oak Run country road. As the sheriff's car continued on with us, I don't have to tell you, I was scared to death. It was very hard for me to drive; I was fidgeting with the radio; on and off, on and off, and I didn't realize it was my nerves and not the radio that was messed up.

"Settle down," I said out loud to myself. [I always talk out loud to myself; well not really, only when a cop is following me with a dead person in the car.] The sheriff's car stayed between us for twenty-two miles through the beautiful fall covered flat fields, up to the beginning of the tall pine and cedar trees that lined the road. I stayed quite a distance behind him, and when I reached the little country store, I saw that the sheriff's car was parked in the parking lot. I could see a policeman sitting in the driver's seat. I drove by slowly and watched in my rearview mirror to see if he was going to follow me.

The next six miles up the winding mountainous road to the property were shear agony for me, as my heart was beating like crazy. All the what-ifs, when's, and whys went though my mind. I thought that maybe I should drive past the entrance gate to the property, in case the sheriff was following me. However, something in my mind kept repeating, "All will be well." I began to relax and felt some comfort in the fact that the sheriff's car wasn't behind me. I drove straight into the gated area. I got out, opened the gate, and parked my car on the other side of it. I closed and locked the gate behind me. There was a hidden key to the gate close by. I sat there until my brother, Henry, came up from below to guard the entrance from unwelcome visitors. He watched for awhile and opened the gate for friends and family. This was the most insane three days of my life. No one could have predicted these events that unfolded into all of this danger and drama.

The family ended up at the property safely with no problems along the way. No one was stopped by anyone. We did keep Henry with his watchful eye on the locked gate. Behind that gate a small graveled winding road led down to a lush green meadow with a small pond below. A little farther down there was a large rustic shop sitting amongst the tall cedar, pine, and fir trees that Dad and the boys had built years before. This was where the service was to be held. For some unknown reason, I felt we were safe here. Even the fact that all six of the vehicles had been followed from the house didn't frighten me anymore. They hadn't come this far. This was where Dad's energy was; it felt safe here. If I drive into that property today, I can still see my dad sitting on the big rock on the front porch smoking his cigarette.

It was a little past noon and the funeral service was scheduled to begin at three o'clock. We had lots to do. The boys—my four brothers—had turned into men with the responsibility they had taken on. They had taken on many-a-brave man's jobs and were all cooperating with each other. They were doing a very good job of it. Together, they unloaded the casket from the ambulance and placed it in the shop on the casket stand. I arranged the flowers and decorations for the service. My sisters set up the chairs and tables for dining after the service. My mother brought many pictures of Dad and the families' outings. She arranged and displayed them on the table next to the casket. She wanted to have the casket open so that people could see how much better Dad looked now than he had for the last few months of his life. The grandchildren and Hester put pictures and little trinkets inside the casket for Dad. They wanted him to take those with him, they said, when he went to heaven. The surprising aspect of the children was that they never had fear of Dad as a dead person as I had when I was young.

Not knowing who would come to the funeral, we set up for a lot of people. I made many personal calls and so did my family. We called most of Dad's close friends, because we didn't trust the service to be advertised in the usual manner of the newspaper. We thought it could result in unwanted trouble. Therefore, his service date and time were left unannounced. I told anyone close to the family if they had people asking about it to give them the information. There was nothing fancy here, and if we needed more room, we could bring in a couple of stumps of wood to set on, and it would have been just right.

Because we did most everything ourselves in preparation for the service, we also officiated ourselves. We played some of Dad's favorite music, and Phoebe read his favorite poem. We said the Lord's Prayer and let friends and family share their memories. Mother spoke of his battles, his strength, his loyalty, and his love. It was a wonderful, happy service and a terrific legacy he left behind. At the conclusion of the service, Si announced that whoever wanted to accompany the family up the hill, to where Dad would be laid to rest, were welcome to come. We left Mother in charge of Dad to give her some time alone. Si led us past the orchard that he and Dad had planted a couple years earlier. Then we went past the big pond with a large dam in front of it, which they had made. There were so many wonderful reminders of Dad here and all his labors. Everyone was so quiet as we walked through the tall trees following Si. I'm sure we were all thinking about Dad. We made a circle and said a prayer together at the site that was to become the family cemetery. What a beautiful setting it was. The pond was filled by a fresh water spring that ran through the property. They had built a platform like a dock that set out in the water for us to swim from in the summer. The dam to the south was big enough that it could be driven across. The pond was lined with tall trees on three sides of it, and the wild flowers bloomed with all of their seasons. It was a lovely, quiet place. Only the birds could be heard rustling in the trees right then. It was the perfect setting. A year later, my brother, Jocko, brought from Idaho a granite rock four feet around, had it cut in half, and made into a head stone with the Simonis name on it. He erected it into cement and placed it at the head of the cemetery to mark Dad's grave and future graves.

We finished the circle with a minute of silence and walked back down the hill. The energy of the group was more light and joyful. The food was ready so everyone began to eat. We enjoyed reminiscing about Dad. After most of the guests had gone, the family stood over Dad in his casket and just looked at him. We were all extremely proud that we had followed through with his wishes. We had achieved together as a family an awesome task. We hadn't asked for this kind of journey, but then sometimes in our lives we're asked to do more than we possibly think possible of ourselves. With all the trials and fears we had gone through to this point, it had turned out better than I could have dreamed. Now as I looked into the casket, I knew that I was looking at my father for the last time. With tears in my eyes and love in my heart, I stared at him. I allowed his image to burn into my memory. I could see such peace in him. I didn't want ever to forget that look. His spirit was there with us. I could feel his energy all around us, as if he were completely enfolding all of us in his arms. He was glad to be home. He was on the land that he worked and loved for the past nine years. The land had given him the strength and the will to live.

I said silently, "I love you, Dad."

And as darkness was beginning to fall, we closed his casket for the last time. There was a tremendous amount of love, peace, and sorrow within the family. I knew he was all right. It had been an honor to care for him in death these last eventful three days. I was proud of the decisions that were made, and I was proud of the family! The experience was so rewarding that it's hard to explain with words what I felt at that moment.

I have a letter from my girlfriend, Jill, who grew up around my household. She saw my dad in all kinds of different situations as she was involved in my family on a daily basis for years. I would like to let you feel what she took away with her twenty-seven years ago, and she says it's very vivid in her memory still today.

When Georgia told me about the book she was writing, I shared with her the impact on me of her father's passing many years before; the family dedication and honorable loyalty to their loved one.

I recall the day of Bob's funeral well, held up in a tiny mountain community, on the family's property that Bob had worked on developing for the whole family to enjoy. It was as though I was looking through a window watching this family. The building that the service was held in was unfinished with a loft apartment above. That day as I waited and watched the service, I could hear the gentle breezes rustling in the tall trees overhead. I could also hear the sound of moving water in the little brook that wound its way down the hillside behind the building. The freshness of mountain air, which surrounded everything, opened my heart and mind to life and the understanding of death. These moments that I sat on a pile of lumber towards the back of the funeral setting, awakened in me the gift that God has given me. The passing of a loved one should be felt as the breeze in the trees—a knowledge that God will care for them. The sound of the running brook is of God's everlasting water. The smell of the mountain freshness, that God will forever replenish everything anew. I've felt from that day forward an inner peace and comfort regarding death. I recall a young man playing his guitar; he had sung the song, "Green, Green Grass of Home," dedicated to Mary (Georgia's mother). He had changed just one line; "hair of raven," instead of "hair of gold" which molded the song about Bob and Mary. There were many others who shared with us their heartfelt times with Bob.

I always thought of Bob as the "Quiet Man."
I asked Phoebe to read a poem that I had written for
Bob, entitled the "Quiet Man."

I will cherish the memory of the love this
family bestowed on their father, and the trials they had
to endure with the passing of their father. Why they
were put through such an ordeal, I cannot understand.
Death does matter, and to have been able to take
part in the love of lives and passing of this family's
member has changed my view of death. For family
to care for their loved ones at the time of death is a
wonderful and natural process called "Love." Thank
you, Georgia, for bringing me into your family, With
Love, Jill

CHAPTER 6
CREMATION

It's amazing what a funeral does for the mind. It gives it the closure that we all need. As I was cleaning up to go home, I knew it was done. This was late October, and as the sun went down, it was getting very cool. I hurried to get finished with the cleanup so that I could get in my car and drive down the hill to town. Some of the men planned to stay the night in the shop; they still had the responsibility of Dad's body to complete. They locked down the shop door for the night and helped us all into our cars. Like a caravan, we all filed up the hill, went out the property gate, and locked it behind us.

The ride home was very surreal. My husband had taken the kids home earlier after the service was over, and I didn't have them to distract my thoughts. I mentally relived the service while driving, thinking to myself how great we as a family had done. I was surprised that I didn't feel like grieving. I actually felt happy and proud. I was proud that we did what our father had asked us and more. Before this, I never could have imagined what it would be like to take care of a dead person for three days and then put on a funeral. We defied the odds and won our battle with all of the obstacles we had against us. It was a fantastic feeling as I smiled to myself. Before I knew it, I was in my driveway. Only the front porch light was left on for me, and I sat there staring with satisfaction. I couldn't believe that I wasn't worried at all about Dad's body being left up there. I just kept hearing in my mind, "All is well."

I don't remember falling to sleep after I went to bed, but I awoke that next morning to a feeling of business as usual. I took care of the baby while my two boys went to school and my husband went back to work. I telephoned my Mother to see if everything was okay. Aunt Cody said Mother was asleep and she was resting well. Everything else was fine, so I tended to some of my personal business that I had neglected for so long. Later that evening, I went to Mother's house. It felt different. She said maybe we could go out for dinner, which she, Cody, Nanny, and I did. Mother told me at dinner that Jocko told her that they had dug a large hole in the early morning hours with a backhoe up by the pond where we had made the circle. They filled it with a cord of dry black oak firewood, and then put Dad's casket on top of that. They covered it with approximately another cord of firewood. Jocko ignited the fire just at daybreak. They said the fire burned very fast, and it was extremely hot. Shortly after the fire burned out, they covered over his grave with dirt.

Now they couldn't have his body. It was one with the earth. The funeral was over, and the cremation and burial was done all at once.

At the first of the next week, the district attorney's office asked that this case be put before the grand jury to see if there was enough evidence or grounds for my family to be charged of any wrongdoing. After extensive research into our case, the grand jury's conclusion was that my family had done nothing wrong. We hadn't done anything unlawful, except not having five dead bodies already in the cemetery, and that was never an issue in the case. My mother now had an official death certificate signed by the doctor that stated my father, Mr. Simonis, had died of pulmonary emphysema and carcinoma of the bladder. With no grounds for their arrest of Si, the charges against him were dropped a couple days after the grand jury's decision.

Chapter 7
Thank You's

My father and his welfare were our main concern. My family and I cared for him around the clock day and night. We provided total care for his every need. After his death, it was not offensive in any way to continue the care of his body. To have an impersonal second-party system to replace our personal loving care of our father, just because of death, was really unthinkable for our family. What we did was not something that we set out to do in this way. Yes, now, it's the only way we handle death in our family.

This experience enlightened our family into a very spiritual adventure that we never expected and it changed my life personally and for us as a family. It has affected each one of us differently. For myself, it made me realize the strength and the power I have to withstand almost anything. It has brought a new meaning of love to the forefront of my existence. It has helped me to somewhat understand what life and death are about. How we treat death should be a huge part of how we live our lives. We will all cross that road someday, and it feels good for me to know where I am going when that happens and who will care for me. If you believe in reincarnation, as I do, then with that belief, only the body dies and the spirit lives on. Therefore, I happily say here that I have to thank Shasta County for the way their officials handled or mishandled my father's death. If it hadn't been for them, I might have never had this chance to receive the gift that death brought to me through the whole episode. I may not have taken this journey that I am on if this hadn't happened. So I say thank you again with all my heart.

Along with this newfound spiritual and physical responsibility, my sister, Mary, found and introduced our family to a wonderful midwife who has devoted her life to delivering babies into this world in the most safe and natural way possible. Deva has assisted me in four home births and over sixty—yes, I said sixty—home births in the twenty-eight years that she has become part of our family. She is what I like to call my earth sister, meaning not born into my family, but we found each other along the way. She's been a godsend to all of us. I personally am very blessed and grateful to have her as my sister and a part of my family. That will be another story!

From the time a life enters this earth, until a life departs it, I will try with complete confidence in myself, to morally and spiritually take full responsibility for myself and my family members. I have learned that all parts of our life matter with death becoming the ultimate end as we see it.

PART FOUR

SHORT STORIES

Here I would like to tell you of others who have died in this family since the death of my father. I'm not going into a lot of detail of their lives or their deaths. In all of these deaths, my family has cared for each of their bodies after their passing. Each body that is kept at home requires dry ice applied to the torso to preserve and prevent decay of the body. We did not cremate any of them ourselves, as we did our father. They were all taken to a crematorium at the appropriate time, which for my family is three days after their death. The family did build all of their coffins and took care of the bodies in their homes until cremation. The family still has that small family cemetery in the mountains nestled in the high trees overlooking that beautiful pond that my dad made. All of their ashes are buried there along with each one's handmade granite headstone in remembrance of their time here.

LITTLE BRANDON

In 1982, one of my sister's, Poni and her husband Michael, lost their precious firstborn child to brain cancer at the tender age of three years old. Little Brandon Thomas was a joyful large child for his age and what a character he had. He was a true delight of a child. During a trip to Hawaii at the age of two-and-a-half, he became ill. He was diagnosed soon after they came home. His parents tried every treatment available medically; some of them brought him some relief but not a cure. Brandon was hospitalized in his last days of life, which through most of it he was comatose. Through different means, Brandon was asked why he was still holding on to life even though the doctors thought he should have died sooner than he did. There were questions asked like was there something holding him here that we didn't know? Through an interpreter, Brandon's reply was that he was just waiting for all of the family members, mostly his cousins, to come to say good-bye to him.

Brandon was in the pediatric wing of the hospital. Children under sixteen years old were not allowed in that department, but they granted our family special permission to see Brandon because of his critical condition. Most all of the kids and the grown-ups of the immediate family went to the hospital on May 29. For some reason, I had not come that day, but I did come with my three kids and my sister, Sookie, and her two kids the next morning on May 30. The kids followed me into Brandon's room where we let them see him for a minute. They said goodbye, and then I escorted them into the hospital play-yard. I returned to the room, and in less than five minutes, Brandon started having difficulty breathing. His mother picked him up from the bed he was on, and cradled him to her chest with his father right there with her. She sat with him in the rocking chair. She rocked him, kissed him, and whispered her love to him. Very soon, he breathed his last breath. That was a very sad day; one of the saddest is when a child dies.

I believe that Brandon was waiting to see all of his cousins to say good-bye. When the last of them came in to see him, it was time for him to leave this earth, and he did.

Brandon was taken by his parents to his home after his death. His father and uncles made him a beautiful child-sized casket. They kept him at their home until his funeral service, and then his parents took him to be cremated.

Brandon not only brought our family joy, but he also brought the staff at the hospital a lot of joy. Some of the nurses said that they see a lot of little kids who are sick and then die, but Brandon got into their hearts. It was incredible how many of the hospital staff showed up for his funeral service at his parent's home.

Brandon was kept in the living room in his casket. When the little kids in the family would go by his casket, they might say something like, "Hi, Brandon" or they'd put a stuffed toy in his casket. Then they'd just go about their business. It wasn't anything different to them as Brandon had been staying in the living room while he was sick. They just figured he was sleeping; they didn't understand that Brandon was sleeping in God's loving hands.

A short time after Brandon's death, I had a dream. My dad came to me in the dream like he was alive. He was sitting on the brick fireplace seat at his home, and he had Brandon next to him nestled under his right arm.

Dad said to me, "He's all right. He's with me."

When I woke up, I knew that this was a message from Dad and I was happy to tell Poni that Dad was there for Brandon when he passed and he'd be taking care of him now.

It left me with such a feeling of satisfaction, and it validated to me that I was still connected to Dad, and also that he and Brandon live on together in the spirit world.

GRANDMOTHER NANNY

My grandmother Nanny, who was very healthy all her life, became ill at the age of eighty-four, and my mother had to have her hospitalized. The family, as always, came together as a strong unit to take care of her. We took around-the-clock shifts while she was in the hospital. Liz was one of Nanny's favorite granddaughters. Liz lived in Alaska at the time but came home immediately when she heard the news that Nanny was sick. Liz spent many night shifts asleep on the hospital floor next to Nanny to care for her.

After ten days in the hospital, Nanny was able to come home. She wasn't really diagnosed with any specific disease except the fact that at her age she was beginning to show some signs of heart failure. She got around pretty good at home after she was released from the hospital, until one morning about a month later. She had a heart attack and died in her bed. It was quite a shock to all of us, especially Margaret and Hester, who found her after she had called out to them. They ran into mother's room to get her. After checking Nanny, Mother called our family doctor, Dr. Jantzen, who had been caring for her. He came to the house and pronounced grandma dead. Then he gave mother a death certificate to be filed with the county. Though we loved our Nanny, her death was not as traumatic as Dad's or baby Brandon's deaths. She was eighty-four, and it could be expected. The family never received a call or heard a word from the authorities regarding us keeping her body. Again, the brothers came together and built her casket as they had done before. The caskets were now becoming more tailored and elaborate. We lined her casket in pink satin, which was Nanny's favorite color. Mother and Aunt Cody made plans for a memorial service to honor Nanny's life at the house with mostly only family and close friends in attendance. My mother, Mary, (Nanny's daughter) made an exquisite blanket of baby pink roses for the top of her casket. After her memorial service, the arrangements were made to take her body to the crematorium the next day. (The family didn't even worry about transporting her body anymore to have her cremated.) The morning of the memorial service the brothers went in to take Nanny in the casket out of her bedroom where we had kept her. We wanted to set it up in the family room for the service, when they discovered that they couldn't get her casket out of the bedroom door without turning it on its side. I know she was dead, but out of respect for our grandmother, they wouldn't turn the casket on its side with her body in it. That's when they decided to dismantle the window. They took both window panes out and two of them went outside while two of them carefully lifted her casket out the window to the other two. We always laughed amongst ourselves at some of the unconventional ways we got things done. My grandmother was such a character that she would have had to laugh herself if she were alive. Many times, she did laugh at herself. The neighbor who was an elderly lady, lived next door to the family for twenty-plus years. She said that after she witnessed this, she thought she had seen everything living next to this family. However, she had to say this was a first. This one took the prize. Taking a casket with their dead grandmother in it out the bedroom window was probably the most bizarre.

MOTHER MARY

What can I say about my mother? What can I say about Mary Simonis that would give you just a glimpse into whom and what she was? I miss her every day of my life. She was the matriarch, and the strong head of my whole big family. She was the glue you could say that held it together. She has been dead for twelve years but my feelings of missing her haven't left me. She was the greatest! Of course, I didn't appreciate her when I was a kid. I was like all kids. Mom was mom and who needed a mom always telling you what to do? Now as a grown-up, I know what a wonderful mother I had. What a truly unbelievable woman she was. She was loving and compassionate, generous and strong, strict when it was required of her, loving, and helpful in every way when we needed her. She was also a very interesting individual. Sometimes she would talk to me about a subject until I couldn't remember or understand what it was she was talking about. Once, I asked her how she knew so much about so many different subjects.

Her answer was, "I read a lot. I listen to what is going on in the world, and sometimes I just know things. I don't know how I know things; I just know them."

When she was a young girl of eleven in 1935, she moved to California from Kentucky with her father, mother, two sisters, and a brother. Her father and mother were divorced. After a couple years, her father left her in charge of her sisters, while he went to Washington state to work. He eventually moved there. She looked after and supported her sisters from the time she was fifteen years old. She always told us her plan was to become a spinster, until she met and married Robert Simonis. No other man could take his place after he died. Then she died of a heart attack on June 17, 1995.

People of all ages loved her; in fact, her nickname was "Mother Mary." She had long, white, curly hair, which she usually wore up on the back of her head, and she had beautiful blue eyes. After having all her children, she still had a slim, sensual figure. She was still as beautiful as an older woman as she was in her younger years. She was mother not only to her thirteen children, but also to all the troubled souls who crossed her path through this life. She always had time and help for them all. She was intuitive and very psychic. One young friend of my sister, Poni, wrote a letter to Mother and presented it to us, the family, at her funeral. It said all and more of who she was. This is what she wrote:

Dear Mary,

I speak not only for myself but for so many others as well, when I say you were like a "second mother" to me. You always had time for me and I always felt welcome in your home day or night. There was always a fresh pot of coffee and plenty of stimulating conversation that gave me, as a girl of sixteen, "food for thought." I learned so much from you. You had a wealth of knowledge about so many things. You had such an easy rapport with all of us young people, who seemed to flock around your home. You always had some well-intentioned advice for us. Bob and you are the people who taught me how to "stand up straight." You could always find something good in everyone; you were so adept at spotting hidden gifts and talents. You looked beyond our hair, our clothes, and our awkwardness, and you saw what we could become. You saw our potential. You had a way of making us feel very special.

You and Bob did more than just "raise" your family; you managed to instill in each one of them something very special—something that definitely sets them apart; some quality about their character, and some integral part of their being that marks them as a "Simonis."

All Simonis' are known for their friendliness, outgoingness, helpfulness, resourcefulness, generosity, cheerfulness, their willingness to work hard, their respect for nature, and their profound spirituality. But the main thing that even a stranger notices right away is that special, quiet self-confidence that they all seem to share.

You demanded much of your children, but from it, they developed self-worth. What greater gift could you have given them than that? You are both deeply loved by your children and grandchildren, and they are all good and gracious people like you and

Bob. The heritage you and Bob have passed down to your children and grandchildren is something very precious; something almost tangible that binds them together in love.

Mary, I have never met anyone like you. You're truly one of a kind. I am very thankful that God allowed our paths to cross in this life. I am a richer person for having known you. Thank you, Mary, for your loving heart and open arms. I want to let you know how grateful I am for all the kindness you have shown me over the years. You touched my life and my heart. You will not be forgotten. I love you.

This really explains who and what my mother was. I find this not only a tribute to Mom and Dad's lives, but to us kids as well. I hope that I can live up to such a legacy.

The last time I saw Mother alive, she was showering in my bathroom. She had stayed with my family and me regularly for the last six months of her life. She had sold the house that I grew up in, and she lived in a small house next door to Poni and Mike. She wasn't the kind of person to be alone; she always had one or more of the grandkids staying over with her. She had experienced a digestive problem a year before dying, which scared her of losing her life. She didn't like to go to bed until the sun came up while she stayed at my house. She always stayed up until two or three in morning most of her life, but this was different. Personally, I think she was afraid of the darkness of night and worried about dying in the dark alone. She seemed to have foreseen her heart attack, because when she showered, she would tell my three-year-old son, Gideon, "to keep an eye on

Grandma," as she put it. As I had heard her saying this to him one day, I asked her not to do that to him.

She said, "Well, I might have a heart attack in the shower."

I told her thinking like that might just bring a heart attack upon her. She had always taught us the power of the spoken word. When I said that to her, she shrugged it off with that funny little expression, like she was a child in trouble. I knew that expression so well, without replying to what I had just said to her. On June 14, I came around the corner and caught her again asking Gideon to "watch Grandma," as she was getting into the shower.

I said, "Mom, please don't do that to him."

Then I took him away from the bathroom.

That evening the family had planned a party at Si's house for my sister Mary's forty-fifth birthday. Mother drove herself to his house in her car. I had already arrived at the party in my car. After being at the party a short time, the phone rang and Mother answered it. It was my sister, Liz; she was frightened and upset over an emergency health problem due to cancer. Mother was so upset over the call that I told her to stay and enjoy the party while I went to see about Liz. Mother had told me only days before while sitting at my kitchen table that she wasn't going to watch her daughter Liz or her sister, Cody, who was also gravely ill, die. So I left the party and went to help Liz. Mother stayed, and all the family had a wonderful time. Liz lived next door to me. After I got to her house and got the situation under control, I called Mother at the party to let her know there was nothing to worry about. Liz, I told her, was okay. I walked down the street to my home around eleven o'clock that evening. I was exhausted and went to bed. The phone rang and I hurried to answer it, thinking it was Liz with another disaster. It was my sister, Mary, the birthday girl.

She said, "Mother just had a heart attack and is on the way to the hospital. She's unconscious. Come right away."

What an unexpected shock to hear that. I dressed and went into my oldest son, Robert's room to tell him that I had to leave the house, and he had to be responsible for his brothers and sister while I was gone.

I will never forget the drive to the hospital alone. It was scary. I was crying, "Not Mother, not Mother! She can't die."

She had always been the pillar of strength for all of us. This couldn't be happening. Surely she would recover. She had been very sick a year before and recovered. I wasn't going to let the negativity of this overcome me. I must remain positive. She would be okay. What would I do without her?

"Oh, please, God, don't let her die," I prayed out loud.

I remember feeling sorry for my kids and all of her grandkids; grandparents are such an enriching part of our lives. I had felt deprived of a father when Dad died and now my mother; this was unthinkable for me. I parked the car, locked the door, and relocked the door, not quite knowing what I was doing. Nothing seemed very clear right then. I just needed to reach Mother.

I went through the emergency room door and went up to the receptionist's window. I asked for the room number that Mrs. Simonis was in, hoping she wasn't dead. The receptionist acted as if she expected me and said that she was in a private section of the emergency room. She said she would get someone to take me there. I didn't realize at that moment that several of my siblings had already arrived before me. While I waited, the time seemed to be standing still until a big man came up to me dressed in regular clothing. He wore a card on a ribbon around his neck that read, "volunteer." He introduced himself to me, and then he took me down several hallways to her room.

As we approached the door, he said, "This is Mrs. Simonis' room," and he turned and left.

I took a deep breath, closed my eyes, and opened the door slowly. I didn't know what to expect to see on the other side of the door. Doctors and nurses were working frantically on Mother. I slipped into the room quietly and stood against the wall next to one of my sisters. Between the doctors and nurses working, I could see glimpses of Mother lying on her back on a gurney-like table in this huge room with tubes and machines connected to her everywhere. It didn't look like her; she was very grey and stiff. Her chest even looked as though it was misshapen, as if it pointed up in a V-shape.

One by one, each one of us kids and our spouses invaded the room except for Liz. My husband was working in Colorado at the time. We lined up against the wall, and we didn't say a word. We just watched the doctors work on her. It was hard to believe that the hospital staff was so accommodating to such a large number of people and allowed us all in the room while the doctors and nurses were working. Mother was connected to machines that were breathing for her. When it looked as though the staff was finished with her, one of the doctors explained to us that she was on life support now.

Another one of the doctors said, "I have to tell you, Mrs. Simonis is not showing any brain activity, but she did have a pulse. We will leave her on life support for twenty-four hours or as long as the family wants her on it."

That was such a shock to hear, but at the same time, I knew that the way Mother's body looked, it wasn't going to be good news. We all agreed that we would keep her connected to the machines, with the hope that a miracle could happen, and Mother might regain consciousness or at least some brain activity. We also agreed that she would not want to be kept alive by machines if there wasn't a chance of recovery. So we left it up to the doctors who said they would know within twenty-four hours if she had a chance of recovering. Then we would have to make the decision if and when to disconnect the machines.

After hearing the unbearable news from the doctor of Mother's prognosis I asked my sister, Mary, what had happened at the party that brought on the attack. She said,

"After most of the family had left the party, Mother went into the kitchen to fix herself a cup of tea; she was standing at the kitchen stove and just collapsed on the floor with a huge thud."

"One of the little grandkids, yelled," "Grandma fell!"

Si was half asleep on the couch when he heard the thud and the yelling. He ran to the kitchen and found Mother on the floor already unconscious and not breathing. Si immediately started CPR on her, and while he was doing that someone called 911. Someone also called my brother-in-law, Mike, who lived next door. He came running over to the house. Si continued the CPR until the paramedics arrived and releaved him. The paramedics took over the CPR and tried for forty-five minutes to get her breathing again. They tried everything on her that they had resources for; trying to simulate some kind of response. It was approximately forty-five minutes that Mother was not breathing. The paramedics couldn't get a pulse or a heart beat on her the whole time. When all of their attempts to revive her had failed, and since she wasn't responding to any treatments, the paramedics stopped everything. They told us that they would be calling the coroner now.

Believe it or not, but at that moment, the paramedic who stayed beside her, said, "I have a heartbeat!"

They all ran back to her and started hitching her up to machines. Without hesitation, they transported her to the hospital.

I chose to believe that with all the trouble the family had when Dad died, Mother was not going to allow a possible repeat of that nightmare if she could help it. I also believe it is a tremendous strain for the soul/spirit to have to go back and re-enter a body after vacating it. But when Mother heard the paramedics use the words, "the coroner," she had to come back into her body to save us, her family, from any trouble we might have had if she just died there and then.

I spent much of my time in the hospital talking with Mother, as if she was awake. I told her that I loved her, and I told her we all wanted her to come back to us if she wanted to and if it was the best thing for her. I even brought her a picture of my son, Kenneth, who had let grandma have his bed for the last six months. I put his photo in front of her bed so she would feel at home if she did regain consciousness. However, nothing we did brought her back. She never regained consciousness or brain activity. So with the doctor's recommendation, we had made the decision together to take her off life support the next evening.

Any kind of news in regards to our family usually got around the town in a hurry. By morning, there were people coming out of the woodwork to see Mother at the hospital. Some were people she hadn't seen for a very long time. With the arrival of more and more visitors, the hospital transferred her into a special private room for everyone's benefit. They were so willing to accommodate our needs. We maintained a vigil by her bedside twenty-four hours a day. There were at least ten to twenty people in her room at any one time. Of course, Mother loved that. She always liked commotion around her. She ran her life at home in that manner, and now she was running her death-bed like that at this hospital.

While at the hospital, we received a call from our loyal friends at our funeral chapel. They had heard the news that Mrs. Simonis was gravely ill, and they wanted to offer their services to our family. They explained that they would drive her body back to the house if we needed them to. They have proven to be truly loyal friends, which was another blessing that we were so grateful for.

One very special memory I have of her death was when Si was sitting next to her bed after the machines had been turned off. She hadn't opened her eyes since the heart attack. Her breathing had become severally labored, and all of a sudden, she opened her eyes and made direct eye contact with Si. As she looked him straight in the eye, a tear fell down her cheek and her eyes closed. She had a special connection with him, and this was her only way to say good-bye to him. I like to say that Mother died two times—once that night at the party when she quit breathing for over forty-five minutes, and then again two-and-a-half days later in the hospital. In my experience with death or birth, I believe whoever is in the room at the time is supposed to be there. Most of us in Mother's room had just stepped out for a break when she stopped breathing. She passed quietly into the other world; a real pillar of strength and goodness passed that day. Soon after she died, I called the funeral home and asked them to come and pick her body up. I didn't want any trouble with the hospital for us to take her out of there. The orderly just wheeled her downstairs after the staff finished with her. He took her to the morgue, and the funeral home attendant was waiting there. Their van took Mother to Si's house. There we cleaned and dressed her for viewing and her memorial service. The men had already started building her casket, and it was almost done. They made a lovely and very feminine casket for her. We lined it with her favorite down comforter. If there was anything in the world that Mother loved, it was beautiful bedding. She supplied all of her children and grandchildren with down comforters. Mother also loved flowers. She made flower arrangements for all occasions and for anyone who asked her. She had made many wedding bouquets for friends and family. For years, she also made flower arrangements for her grandchildren to sell at a local restaurant in town. She never accepted any money. She wasn't only called "Mother Mary," but she was also called, "The Flower Lady." That's why we decided that she needed to leave this earth with as many flowers as we could get our hands on for her. I had a florist at the time so we not only had flowers everywhere at her service, but all of our family and guests filled her casket with flowers when her service was over. We thought it would be a very lovely and fitting end for "Mother Mary, The Flower Lady."

At the funeral, my daughter, Georgianna, came up to me after the service and asked me a question.

"Mom, what happened at the hospital with Grandma?"

Not knowing exactly what she was referring to, I questioned her about what she was asking me. It soon became clear to me that I needed to know why she was asking the question. I discovered that Trece, a friend who had been involved in our family her whole life, had relayed a message to me about what she had spiritually received from Mother's bedside while she was visiting Mother in the hospital. Apparently, Trece had given me the message at the time she received it at the hospital, but it didn't register with me at the time. So I went to find Trece to have her explain what she had told me in the hospital again. I found her in a crowd of people.

We hugged each other and I said to her, "Trece, please tell me what the message was you had for me in the hospital from Mother."

She was just beaming and anxious to tell me.

She said, "Remember when I went to see Mary the first night she was in the hospital? You came in the hospital room and I was already there with other family members. I was so excited to tell you that your mother's spirit was alive, and she was here in the room. She was introducing each one of us in the room to some kind of an audience of people or entities. I even felt my hair move like a light breeze had blown through it when I arrived," she said. "I saw your mom standing there by the bed; she touched my hair and introduced me to whomever it was she was introducing us to. Your mom wants me to let you know that she is very happy and very proud of her family. She is also very happy to be back home with whomever it is she is with." Then Trece said, "Your dad was there, too, standing on the other side of her bed against the wall with that smile on his face. He was patiently waiting for your mother to finish talking, as he always did."

I was astounded, yet I believed every word of what Trece was telling me. She was the child that I was babysitting when I was twelve years old. I had been around her all of her life. She wouldn't lie or make a story like that up.

In fact, Mother always said, "Trece is special. She has the sight!"

I then asked her, "Do Mom and Dad look like they did in the pictures we had of them on her casket?"

"No, they looked like they were in their mid-forties," she said.

This was so exciting to me; it was weird that I didn't remember Trece telling me about this at the hospital. However, there was always so much confusion in the room that I understood why I didn't get it then. I asked her how she saw what she had seen.

She said, "It's like watching a movie or something like that. It's something I see in a flash and I know the whole scene."

I hugged Trece again and said, "Thank you."

I now felt very thankful and relieved to know that Mom and Dad were there for each other, and that they were together again.

I don't think you get over the death of a mother. Life without my mother would be a real challenge for me now. I depended on her advice, her love, and her presence in my life and my children's lives. I never imagined she would die so soon. I saw her almost every day and traveled many places with her; I miss her wisdom and company each day of my life.

Mother's funeral was held at Si's house in the backyard. Many of our county's top officials attended her service to show their respect for this figure of community strength. The sheriff, who was one of many of her friends, asked to be the first to sign her memorial book.

The county's position towards the family on taking care of deceased family members by their family, must have changed by now, since not a word was said to any member of my family as to if we had a death certificate or not. They also didn't inquire about what would become of her remains; no one bothered us.

The day after Mother's funeral, I was attending to some of Mother's business. I looked at her purse lying on my kitchen counter. I thought to myself, Mother never let her purse out of her sight. Even when she went to bed, she would put it on her nightstand next to her. That's when I thought that all the material things we have in our lives mean nothing to us when we die and leave this earth. It hit me like a bolt of lighting. It was the realization that the only thing we can take with us is love and our actions that we've created throughout our time here. Since then, I have tried to live my life remembering "Mother's purse."

OLD FRIENDS

At approximately seven in the evening, I received a telephone call from my girlfriend, Jill.

She said, "Hi, what are you doing?"

"I'm just getting dinner," was my reply.

She sounded a little strange and said, "Clyde just passed away a few minutes ago. He was under hospice care, you know." (Clyde was her ex father-in-law who was in his eighties.

"What?" I said.

I had known he was sick, but I had seen him just a week before at the bank. I didn't realize he was that sick.

Jill said, "April asked me to call you to see if you could come over and help us fix Clyde's body for burial."

April was Clyde's wife of sixty years.

She continued, "She wants him to be home for awhile longer, but doesn't want him to be left as he died."

This was a shocking request to say the least! I had known these two elderly people for twenty years. They weren't strangers to me, yet it was an odd request, since they weren't my family. I didn't think this was something I could do. I tried everything that I could think of to get out of it. It's one thing to be dealing with your own family's loved one's death and body, but someone else's, well, that's just not something that I wanted to do.

I kept saying to Jill, "No, I don't think I can do that. Oh, I don't think I can do it. Jill. I really don't know what to do. You guys can do the same thing I could do."

Finally, after many tearful pleads from April, I gave in and said I would be over to see if I could help. My intention was just to go over for moral support for Jill.

I told Jill, "Go to the grocery store and buy some dry ice. I'll meet you back at Clyde's house."

The only people there at the house when I arrived were April, Jill, Clyde, and Jill's new husband, Sonny. I thought, "Where are his children? Where are the immediate family members?" He and April had three children. One had passed away as a young child, and the other two lived out of state. I found out later that they were on their way there.

April hugged and thanked me for coming when I came in, I felt so sorry for her.

She was crying and said, "He said he wouldn't leave me. What will I do without him?"

She was so pitiful sitting in her chair with her dead husband in the hospital bed across the room from her. I had to do the best I could to help her feel better about her husband's death. I talked to her for a few minutes. Then I looked at the situation and rolled my eyes at Jill. I told April I would see what I could do.

Jill, Sonny, and I straightened Clyde's body and changed his clothes. The whole time I thought to myself that I couldn't believe

I was doing this. Mostly, I was directing Sonny how to do most of the work.

While we were redressing him in the outfit of clothes April had for him, I said in a whisper to Jill and Sonny, "Don't you guys think something is wrong with this picture? Jill, you're the ex daughter-in-law. This is your new husband, and I'm just a friend. What are any of us doing here?"

Well, that broke the tension in the room, and we all started to laugh. Out of respect for April, it took everything in our power to keep from laughing out loud because April was sitting right behind us. Of course, we didn't want to upset her anymore than she already was, but it sure made us feel better to laugh.

April was so grateful at seeing her husband looking better; she called the funeral chapel the next day to come and pick up Clyde.

April sent me a thank you note saying it was extremely helpful to her to be able to release Clyde, knowing people who cared about him took care of him for the last time. She said the next day that it seemed right to let him go. Four months later, and after sixty years together, she followed him to the other side.

ALL ABOUT LIZ

My sister, Liz, and I went into the floral business together in 1992. Liz had lived in Alaska for eight years and had come home to settle down around her family to have her daughter. We lived next door to one another, and we both had a small child. Our business and private lives worked very well together. Liz was just about the most funny and the liveliest one of all the Simonis kids. She lived a full life in the forty years she was here on this earth. In 1996, she was diagnosed with cervical cancer. She tried many different medical and homeopathic treatments, even going out of the country for treatment. She was determined that she would beat this dis-ease in her body. No one could tell her any different, and if they tried, she cut them off. That wasn't in her nature, but that was how determined she was about getting well. In February 1998, she lost her painful battle and passed away. She was under hospice care in her home at the time of her death. I ran [literally ran up the street] to her aid from my house many, many times over the last year of her life with one emergency after another. But on this February morning, she called me crying in pain, saying she was hemorrhaging. I flew up the street to her; she was in danger of dying. I asked her if she wanted me to call the hospital or if I should call the hospice people. We had set up a call system with them in the event that something like this might happen. She thought for a minute and asked me what she should do. I told her she must make the decision for herself. I couldn't decide that for her. She decided that I should call for the hospice. I called the hospice people who came immediately to help me. What a wonderful organization they are. They helped me get her on track. We got the bleeding stopped. Then we decided what the next move was to be, which was to get her pain under control. Then we followed through with her decision to stay at home. I called the family for help and support as this was a tremendous decision for Liz to have to make. Her daughter was only seven years old, and she didn't want to leave her.

She had slipped into a semi-coma; the family was maintaining a twenty-four hour vigil the last three days at her bedside. I had to go down the street to my house at three in the morning. The rain was coming down so hard at that time, it was just a deluge of water falling. It had rained everyday since the first day of the New Year. Then suddenly, the rain stopped as I came out of my house to walk back to Liz's house. The sky opened up and cleared rapidly. I stopped to watch the stars twinkle with a rhythm all their own that made me feel amazed and happy. I had felt so sad a few minutes earlier. Now I felt so good coming back into Liz's house. Then I realized the family was all in her bedroom, and she was dying. I rushed to her bedside and watched as she struggled for her last breath; passing away right then. The sky opened up for her entry at that moment, and I was amazed that I got to see it.

Sandy, a close friend of the family, had always been there to help us in times of crisis. Now she was in the process of making Liz a white linen gown for her passing. I called her later that morning, and she came over to help dress Liz. After Sandy dressed her in the beautiful handmade gown, she and I fixed her on her bed until the men could get her casket made. Liz was a crystal fanatic; she had crystals hanging all over her house. At around ten o'clock the next morning, I was cleaning the house with some of the other family members. That's when I noticed a very peculiar rainbow illuminating up the center of Liz's feet as she lay in the middle of her bed. I called to the others and we watched as the sun moved across the window. The rainbow moved straight up the center of Liz's body, and then up through and over the top of her head. The rainbow looked like it came out of the crown of her head. To me, this was Liz's way of letting me know that she was all right; her spirit was free and alive.

You see, when Liz was a young girl, she had given Mother a card that hung on Mother's bulletin board by the telephone that read, "I believe in God because of rainbows." That was confirmation enough for me. This was a sign to let me know she was all right, because we had talked about the afterlife so many times before. So since I knew she was all right, why did she have to come to me two times in the night after that and actually sit on the end of my bed? It was very late the first time it happened. I was reading in bed and dozing off. I reached up, turned off the light, and nestled down into the covers. All of a sudden, I felt someone sit on the end of my bed. I was scared stiff; I thought that maybe someone had been hiding in my bedroom. I lay very still for a minute wondering who could be in the room with me. It took some courage for me to jump up and turn on the light, but when I did, no one was there. I got out of bed and checked the whole house, going room to room. Now I was questioning my sanity. "Was I imagining it?" Well, I didn't imagine it, because a couple of nights later the exact same thing happened to me. This time I had been thinking about when it had happened before and decided it was Liz just checking in. I addressed her by name.

I said, "Liz, I know it's you, and if you're here to check on Lilly, she's well and loved."

It didn't frighten me this time. I never turned on the light, and soon the pressure released itself from the foot of my bed. It was as if she said, "Okay," and left. It happened one more time about a year later, and I just acknowledged that I knew she was there by saying her name. Now it has been nine years since she passed away, and I haven't had another visit from her, but Lilly has. (Lilly is Liz's daughter who lives with me, and she does come quite frequently to check on her.)

This time the men went all out on building Liz's casket. They made her a beautiful hardwood coffin with a see-though Plexiglas top that was fit for a princess. Liz had such a sense of humor. She was a funny, wonderful sister and person. The brothers figured she would have gotten a real kick out of it. She is missed very much.

The weather was cold and beautiful the three days after she passed. On the day of the funeral, it started to rain again and never let up for another month. I like to think that Liz cleared the sky the day she left us!

TRUE LOVE

I was awakened by a phone call from my sister-in-law, Melinda, about six o'clock on the morning of September 28, 2001. She was so upset and said that her son, Daniel, and his girlfriend, Kayla, had been in a car accident the night before. Both of them were killed. When you hear this kind of news, your whole world stops, and you're in utter disbelief. This can't be true. Two young people who are vibrate, young, and alive one minute, are dead the next. No! They were nineteen and eighteen years old. On the evening before, Melinda said that she came home just as they were leaving the house. Daniel was getting into the passenger side of the car. That's when Melinda said she noticed how "cute" he looked and told him so. She said he seemed to be just glowing as he got into the car and drove away. That would be the last time she would see either of them alive. Daniel had told his mother that they were going to a concert seventy miles away, and they'd probably be home late. When they left, they went into town and had dinner at a Chinese restaurant where my sister Mary worked. Mary served them dinner, and they told her they were going to a concert. When they left the restaurant, for reasons unknown to anyone, they went east on the freeway back towards Daniel's house instead of south, the direction where the concert was. They were killed a few minutes later on the freeway. The investigation that was conducted by the police has never been able to give a cause for the accident.

I live in the mountains, which is twenty-five minutes away from their home. I told Melinda that I would be right down. I carefully hurried down the hill with thoughts going through my head. One of my most distinct thoughts was my concern for my son, Douglas. He was the same age as Daniel and was usually his constant companion since they were babies. I remember thinking, "Where's Douglas?" I was so worried that if he heard this news from someone else, I didn't know what might happen to him. I felt like I needed to be the one to tell him. I was wrong. At his age, I think he had much more support from his friends who knew them both. When I arrived at their house, the family was assembling again. In an emergency, everything stops, and the family rallies together for the support of all the events that must follow. We all knew our specialties, and we put them into action when needed.

These beautiful young people were killed on Friday night. They were taken to the hospital, pronounced dead, and then were taken to the county morgue, which was closed for the weekend. This was very upsetting news to the family. Not only had Daniel died, but also his family wasn't allowed to see or verify that the body was his body for two more days. His mother and father needed more proof of his death than a policeman at their door at one o'clock in the morning telling them that their child had been killed in a car accident at approximately eight o'clock in the evening. It was terrible for them to have their son kept from them. The weekend crept by, but it gave the family time to prepare for the funeral service. Daniel's father and four brothers began the sorrowful task of building the caskets—one for Daniel and one for Kayla. Daniel's mother and sisters lined the caskets with a light, beautiful linen material. (Kayla's family was having their own service for her.)

Daniel's body was released from the county morgue to the funeral chapel on Monday, October 1. His father brought his son home in the handmade casket. The funeral was scheduled for the following day at the family's home. Since these two young people were in love, his family wanted to celebrate their lives and try to make it as joyous as possible. Because of their ages, we had expected many, many young people along with maybe hundreds of other people. The service was to honor both Daniel and Kayla.

Under the oak trees in the family's backyard, the caskets were set up with their individual pictures on top of their own caskets. To our amazement and joy, more than 600 guests came to the funeral service. People were everywhere. As the service got underway, people were invited to tell their individual stories. Aunt Hester got up to speak, and as she did, she had asked two of the little girls in the family to release two white doves that she brought to the service to symbolize the love between these two young people. As they were released and Hester spoke, the white doves took flight over the crowd. One landed on a branch of the oak tree positioned over the top of Kayla's casket, while the other dove went straight to Daniel's mother, Melinda. Several times it circled her head as Hester was speaking. It then flew to the oak tree and landed on a branch directly over Daniel's casket. The birds stayed there throughout the service, except the dove that was over Daniel's casket kept flying back to Melinda and then back to his same branch. This was very comforting to all of us to see these birds reacting in this manner. It gave us a chance to believe that these two spirits live on and these birds symbolized this. It was perhaps a reflection of that belief!

Living in the mountains sometimes gives me a lot of time to myself. When spirit hits me, I usually stop and react to an idea in my mind. A couple months after Daniel's death, I was playing cards alone one night. While I was shuffling the deck of cards, I looked up. On my mirror was the picture of Daniel from his funeral. It seemed to be saying something to me.

I looked at it for a minute and then said, "All right, Daniel, I will read the cards for you."

I have played with reading cards for years. It is a tradition that my grandmother did, and passed it to my mother, who in turn passed it to me. I have only read cards for family and close friends, usually for fun at a holiday function. However, for some reason, I was to read for my dead nephew. That was something that had never even crossed my mind before. As I dealt and read the cards, I was infused with thoughts of what the cards were saying to me. Many times my predictions have come true in a sense. As I laid out the cards that night, I believe Daniel came through and told me of his accident. The cards said he had completed his time here, and he now had a mission that he and Kayla were on that they had to do together. The cards showed me that his mother and father would miss him, but their love would get them through this hard time. The cards said he and Kayla were married, happy, and very busy. I was so excited with what the cards told me that I wrote it all down. The next day I called his mother to deliver this warm positive message to her.

How do I read these cards? I really don't know. It's just the way they lay out and the interpretation and feelings that I get from each card that give me an idea of what they say.

A Young Rose

It was a beautiful morning in November 2005. Several of my sisters and I had met early that morning at my sister Phoebe's home for scones and coffee. We try to do that before the hustle of the holiday season starts each year. After finishing breakfast, Mary was the first to leave the get-together. The telephone rang as we were all readying ourselves to depart. It was Mary. Phoebe answered, and she listened for a moment. As I was looking at her, I could see a dreadful look come over her face.

She blurted out, "Oh my God! Malia was killed in a car wreck."

"What? What?" I said in utter disbelief.

How could this be happening again in our family?

I fell to the floor crying and repeating, "Not again. What is this all about? What is this all about? What is the use?"

How can I comprehend this? How can anyone? My thoughts went then to Malia. Poor little Malia Rose. She was only twenty-three and a lovely young lady who never caused a bit of trouble. We hardly knew she was around most of the time. She never demanded much attention from life. She was a very sweet and beautiful girl. My thoughts went to her parents. I couldn't imagine their grief. They had already lost their firstborn son years before and now their only daughter. This can't be real! What kind of a test of their sanity is this?

Phoebe had hung up the phone, and I had all these thoughts and questions in my head. Is this true? If so, where is Malia? What about her parents and brothers? I felt as if I needed to call my sister before rushing out of her house. I picked up the telephone to call and my heart sank. How do I make that kind of call? How do I ask my sister if her child was just killed? I put the phone down, and I waited a few minutes to try to compose my feelings. I slowly picked the phone back up and dialed the number. Part of me wished that it wouldn't be answered, but my sister, Poni, answered. My heart broke for her. I tried to speak without falling apart.

I asked her, "What is this that I am hearing, and is it true about Malia?"

She replied, controlled and almost robotically, "Yes, it's true; Malia was killed in a violent single car accident about one o'clock this morning. She was coming home from her aunt's house."

"Oh, my God. Where is Malia now?" I said.

She said, "At the funeral chapel."

I couldn't talk anymore except to say I would come right out to her house.

The parade of people who came through their house that day and the days to follow was incredible. There were so many young people; all not knowing how to react to such a wasteful tragedy. Poni and Mike were extremely well-equipped to comfort these young people with their tender love and caring for all. Poni's home is very much like our parent's home was, the young people have always flocked to it.

Later in the afternoon, Poni asked some of us [sisters] to go with her to the funeral chapel to see Malia. Of course, I said I would go with her. She had expressed her wishes to the funeral director through our sister, Hester. She didn't want anything done to Malia's body until she saw her. The funeral director followed Poni's wishes with whatever she needed. They made Malia look as presentable as possible when we arrived and that was greatly appreciated. This funeral chapel has always been there for our family with their excellent judgment, compassion, service, and help.

It was about four o'clock when we arrived at the funeral chapel. All eight of us girls approached the double front doors as the owner met us. He escorted us into where he had Malia laying. She was on a gurney wrapped in a sheet that went under her arms and covered her to her knees. My first impression at seeing Malia, I will never forget, was her beautiful long slim arms and legs. It made me think of when she was born. I was there at her home birth, and everyone's first reaction was of her long arms and legs. She had such a beautiful body. As I walked around the gurney in front of her, I couldn't help but to say out loud how beautiful she appeared. She looked young, innocent, and asleep-like. Poni went straight to Malia. She cradled her face in her hands and kissed her. She brushed her hair back from her face. Then she lovingly kissed Malia again and again and cried. We all circled around this beautiful young lady, as we wept. It was a very emotional visit for all of us. The room was very comfortable and the energy felt okay. We held hands trying to calm ourselves and recited the Lord's Prayer together. Amazingly, Malia only seemed to have some scratches visible on her neck. We stayed with Malia for some time. We told stories of the years gone by and her most recent adventures. To be able to see and touch your loved one, stops the questions. It gives a sense of satisfaction, even in death, visibly to know that it is true they are dead, no matter how much we wish it wasn't so; no matter how much it hurts, and it does hurt.

Poni decided to leave Malia there that evening until Malia's father and her brothers could build her a coffin, and then she would bring her home.

I decided after leaving the funeral chapel to go home also. This was such an emotionally exhausting day that I hoped I'd never have to repeat. The next morning, I awoke to an annoying voice, a question, going through my mind. I kept trying to ignore it and sleep more, but the voice would repeat, again and again the same thing in my mind—What do we do when someone goes?—I finally had to acknowledge that spirit was pushing me to get up and write this down on paper. I went to my kitchen, took out paper and pen, and to my surprise, the pen started scribbling across the page with remarkable speed. I wrote:

> What do we do when somebody goes?
> We've got lots of ideas, but nobody knows.
> Where do we go and what do we do?
>
> Only God knows; it's all so new.
> We'll miss them, wonder, and ask why?
> All of our answers lie up in the sky.
>
> A beautiful soul will fly today.
> God, please help them on their way.
> I know you're there to help them along,
> While also you're there for us, to help us be strong.
> We love you, Lea.

I was amazed. I have heard of spirit coming through people like this, but I had never experienced it or been prone to poetry. So I thought I'd copy this on a pretty card and give it to my sister today. I rewrote it all very nice, put it in an envelope, and went about my daily morning affairs. An hour later, I was outside feeding my dogs when the voice in my head returned and overtook me. This time I couldn't ignore it. I dropped everything I was doing and ran into my house. The paper I had written the original poem on was on the island in the kitchen. I turned the paper over, and the pen began scribbling again. I wrote:

> Don't feel sorry for me today,
> There are millions of projects—I'm on my way.
> I came for awhile and left them undone.
> Today I'll start on number one.
>
> Be happy for me.
> Sorry I didn't say "Goodbye,"
> But if you know me, you know why.
> I love you all. Take care of Magoo.
> Remember, I will always be with you. ~ Malia

I believe in my heart that the first poem came through me from spirit. I was so upset and I had all those questions in my mind the day and night before. But this second one, this wasn't mine. Malia's spirit came through me that morning to answer some of the questions I had been struggling with—all the whys I had been asking myself.

No one can tell me that the spirit doesn't live on when the body dies. I felt it, and I saw the magic of the pen gliding across the paper in my hand. It relayed the message through me to be given to her mother, father, brothers and anyone else who would listen.

I rewrote the card for my sister and included Malia's message of love and duties she was to fulfill. When I told Poni how the poem had come to me, she was sure that the way it was written that it had to have come directly from Malia.

By the way, if you're wondering who "Magoo" is, he is Malia's little black pug dog who was in the car with her at the time of the accident. Magoo was not injured and was returned home safely that morning to Malia's family.

ECLIPSE

In my personal experiences of attending to my family's departed loved ones, they have all, in one way or another, let me know that their spirit lives on. They have different missions to be completed somewhere else. Is it the other side as we call it? Maybe, I really don't know where it is, but I do know that the spirit is alive and well wherever it is that we go after we leave this vehicle that we call our body.

There will be people who will read this that will connect and know exactly what I'm saying. To them, they will know this is true. There will also be people who will be skeptical and may not believe any of it. We will always have the questions and the conflicts. My hope is for the ones who have had spiritual experiences similar to mine that they are not afraid of death. It is the ongoing part of life that, if treated in that manner, is very essential to life. I'm not here to make you believe as I believe; I am only here to tell my personal life-changing experiences. I hope that you will enjoy my story, and that it will bring some comfort to each person who has had loved ones pass.

I believe there are two things that bind people together and will draw them to each other if parted, as in death. One is Karmic Law and the other is the Law of Love. There is no self-will or man-made mandate that is powerful enough to part those who are karmically bound together in love, and this bond is so strong that even death cannot sever it. We frequently ask, "Will those who have been together in life, as for instance, husband and wife, children and parents, friends and relatives, meet and know each other after death parts them?" I believe the answer is simple; if there is a bond of real love between them, then nothing on earth or in heaven, the other side or wherever, can keep them apart. They will meet again and the old bond will be resumed. Love is the law of nature. It's the one and only eternal law, and no force is strong enough to permanently interfere with its functioning.

It was only seventy or eighty years ago that most people took care of their own dead in their homes. We now live in a different world that is a very fast-paced society, so it's not conducive to our lifestyles to take on the responsibilities of taking care of our dead loved ones when they die. I also understand that some people might not want that responsibility.

However, for my family, and me, we choose to care for our dead loved ones. It allows us to begin a healing process that I don't believe happens as quickly or as efficiently as when you just see them dead. Then a couple days later, you have a funeral. Either they are there in a casket, or if they were cremated, only their ashes and a picture would be there.

In my floral business, I know many times that people will express the need to spend a little more money on funeral flowers. They go the extra mile to honor the deceased person, as it is the last earthly gesture they can offer to them. By knowing the deceased loved one and preparing their body, this offers a special satisfaction that brings comfort to the living. They know this is exactly the way the deceased would want their death carried out.

The ending of our lives should be as important as the beginning; just, of course, in a different manner. My belief is life does go on after death, even though we sometimes don't think so, or we can't see it.

The first day when you hear that someone close to you has died, even in the advent that death was expected, there is SHOCK— an unbelievable shock. I think there is a strong fear factor about death that paralyzes our thinking. We don't think right. We run on emotion—sometimes we can't run at all. We feel lost; we sometimes cannot comprehend how we can go on living. We might ask ourselves what life will be without this person or that person. When a child dies, we can't fathom a reason why. We think they should have a whole lifetime ahead of them. In addition, if it is your child (through my personal experience), a part of you dies, too. Your heart is never the same again, no matter what the child's age might be. All parents, in my opinion, would change places with their child in a minute, if only they could just see them alive again or speak to them one more time. With our grief, also comes our guilt; if only I had told him/her that I loved them more; or maybe spent more time with them; or the last time I saw them, I could have spent more time with them; or I didn't say enough; or I wish I would have gotten there before they died. I will never forgive myself. The list of guilt goes on and on. You can torture yourself for years or sometimes even a lifetime.

By the second day after a death, you begin questioning life. What is it all about? You can't really accept or believe that your loved one is really dead. You find yourself expecting them to walk through the door, call on the phone or in my case, just wake up. It just does not register in your mind; it doesn't seem real at this time that they are really dead.

But by the third day of caring for and seeing your dead, loved one's body, you understand. You realize that that person is really dead. You know that the body that you have been lovingly caring for is now only an empty shell. Its purpose was to house the spirit or the life force, as I like to call it. It becomes clear to you that that life force is not in that body anymore.

When that realization happens to you, and you experience this wonderful transformation that you can't do anything about, something inside of you begins a healing process. Your heart lightens and your spirit becomes (somewhat in a strange way) accepting that everything is okay and in its own time. You know that your loved one is all right, that you have done the best you could for them, and you will be all right, too. By no means am I saying you won't be saddened, that tears won't continue because of the loss, but in all of my experiences, I have accepted the death (again in an odd way) better by taking care of my own family's last wishes, than by relinquishing them to someone else's care.

When the events that unfolded with my father's death forced my family into this unconventional behavior, it opened my eyes as well as my family's eyes and mind. It gave us a more balanced feeling of life and death, and it created a love in our hearts. We felt a personal responsibility towards all matters that had to do with family that we could not ignore. Our actions were not our intended or original choice. Neither was the outcome our intention. But after all that had transpired, I now would not have it any other way. In all aspects of this life, to me, death as well as birth matters.

Death Matters!